GREAT
CHRISTIAN
PRAYERS

GREAT CHRISTIAN PRAYERS

From Two Thousand Years of Christian Faith

Compiled and edited by
LOUISE AND R. T. KENDALL

Hodder & Stoughton
LONDON   SYDNEY   AUCKLAND

British Library Cataloguing in Publication Data
A record for this book is available from the British Library

ISBN 0 340 75609 8

Typeset in Monotype Fournier by
Strathmore Publishing Services, London N7

Printed and bound in Great Britain by
Clays Ltd, St Ives PLC

Hodder & Stoughton
A Division of Hodder Headline Ltd
338 Euston Road
London NW1 3BH

Contents

Foreword

There are three stages in prayer. The first is basically 'God bless me, Mummy and Daddy', with a shopping list to a God who is there to deliver our wishes. The second is once we have come alive to the Lord Jesus as our Saviour. The Holy Spirit brings us into a personal relationship and prayer normally moves into worship, conversation, sharing and desiring God's will although remnants of the first sort of praying can sadly linger and confuse. The third is when we begin to hunger and thirst for God, to become like St Paul when he longs to know Christ, the power of his resurrection and the fellowship of his sufferings. Here prayer starts to explore the deep wonders of God in devotion and worship as well as in far more comprehensive intercession. This is where this marvellous book takes us.

When Louise Kendall talked about her exploration into the prayers of Christians across the centuries, her passion, excitement and deepened devotion to God glowed from her heart. She had been ready to explore the prayers of saints who had different Christian affiliations and found the throb of her own heart matching theirs. Although extempore prayer is still integral to her prayer life, she discovered that in written prayers there could be gathered expressions of deep devotion, phrases with profound insight, and a range of confession, worship, and intercession that left much extempore praying in the fading shadows.

That Louise and R.T. have now turned that great discovery into this book is a gift to the whole church. Not all the prayers will ring bells with us but most will strike an inner chord and will come to be part of our own prayer life in years to come. We move over the centuries with prayers from Augustine, Corrie ten Boom, Newman, Campolo, Luther, Chalke, Lancelot Andrewes (who blew my prayer life into new orbits) and so many others. Our hearts are warmed by Timothy Dudley-Smith's beautifully poetic yet insightful prayers, with glorious phrases like 'the choir of stars'. I am so glad that the prayer (17 Feb) of the confederate soldier just before he died in the battle of Richmond is here, as I use it frequently and whenever I quote it everyone wants a copy ... it is penetratingly moving. You will want to mark the prayers that stand out for you as you use the book across a year and then return to embrace them as part of your own devotion. It will help us all to move deeper into true prayer to our glorious Lord. For all the passion, research and hard work that has gone into this gem of a book we are all in the debt of two very special people ... Louise and 'R. T.' Kendall.

RT REVD DR MICHAEL A. BAUGHEN
Bishop of Chester 1982 to 1996
Rector of All Souls, Langham Place, London 1970 to 1982

Preface

On Christmas Day 1998 I gave my wife Louise an old copy of *Great Souls at Prayer* (1898), ancient prayers selected and arranged by Mrs Mary W. Tileston. Some months before, Robert and Beth Amess loaned Louise their only copy, but she wanted one of her own. A few weeks before Christmas I began looking high and low in London for this book. Two days before Christmas I was given a tip that Pendlebury's, a second-hand bookshop near Seven Sisters in London, might have a copy. They did. It cost me only £3, but you would have thought I had given Louise a gold necklace when she opened that present! She wept. Having a liturgical background has given her a love for ancient prayers, and Robert and Beth's copy had formed part of her daily devotions.

You can imagine my astonishment when, out of the blue less than a month later, David Moloney of Hodder & Stoughton asked me to compile a book of prayers which they suggested calling *Great Christian Prayers*. I immediately replied, 'Louise can do that – that will be her book.'

And so it is – this is really Louise's book. She has done all the hard work – the research and the editing. My role has mainly been to contact some contemporary Christian leaders to see if they too would like to have a part in this book. Most have responded with at least one prayer. Those who declined said they didn't write out their own prayers. I pushed a few of them to give it a try anyway – and it worked. David Yonggi Cho's secretary kindly took one of his public prayers from a tape recorder and translated it for us. So many of the prayers by Christians still living have a story of their own. It is Louise, though, who is responsible for the choice of the old prayers that constitute the bulk of this book.

The prayer attributed to George Washington may or may not have been written by him, but he certainly prayed it as it was found in his own handwriting among his papers. In December 1994 I asked Rodney Howard-Browne if he would come to Westminster Chapel on a Saturday morning and pray in the pulpit (with no-one present) and then pray for Louise. This is described in *The Anointing: Yesterday, Today, Tomorrow* (Hodder & Stoughton, 1998). For over three years Louise suffered from a very serious condition that was instantly healed that day when Rodney and his wife Adonica laid their hands on her and prayed for her. The prayer Rodney prayed in the pulpit moments before was actually a written prayer that came out of the Welsh Revival. The memory of that day makes the prayer doubly special to us.

You might also like to read Billy Graham's response to this book:

> You and Louise have taken on a big task to pull together a book of prayers from throughout history. I do not feel qualified to be a part of such a book, but if you have a suitable spot for it – the prayer which I have perhaps been the most well-known for is that prayed at the end of every one of

our Crusade meetings around the world as we invite people to receive Christ as Saviour and Lord.

Because this is so basic and simple, I doubt that this is the kind of prayer you had in mind, but I submit it for your consideration since it epitomises our entire ministry through all these years, and is the first prayer that many people ever pray as they reach out to God and begin a new life with Him.

We immediately decided that Billy's prayer should come on 1 January, alongside Dr George Carey's New Year's prayer.

We sincerely thank all those Christian leaders who have responded to our plea to share some of their prayers. I want to thank the family of Karl Barth, who have provided prayers never before published. In the case of these various Christian leaders, you will see how their prayers mirror their own ministry, situation or suffering. It seems to me that their contributions have added wonderfully to our book and we thank them sincerely.

There are some people who deserve our very deepest thanks. We begin with the Evangelical Library, where Louise spent a lot of time and which has loaned her not a few books. Our thanks go also to the Theological Library of King's College, London. We thank Victor Wong for sending the prayer that came out of China. Although sadly lost in the post, we thank J. John for sending his collection of Greek Orthodox prayers. Maurice Rowlandson has supplied names of a few British Christians I might not have thought of. Celia Bowring has helped Louise edit some of the prayers, and Lady Elizabeth Catherwood has been helpful in editing some of the great prayers of her father, Dr D. Martyn Lloyd-Jones.

I thank Brian Reed, my assistant, who kindly took responsibility for compiling a Glossary – no mean task. When he handed me the finished product I found myself riveted; it reads like a *Who's Who* in the Christian Church! My secretary Sheila Penton has worked with Louise and me throughout the period spent preparing this volume. We especially appreciate the encouragement of David Moloney, our Editor, and also that of Charles Nettleton, Director of Hodder & Stoughton.

This book is lovingly dedicated to Louise's mother, Mrs Orville Hess, now eighty-six and living in Boise, Idaho. Thank you, Mother, for all you continue to mean to us.

R. T. KENDALL
London, March 2000

Introduction

Those who do not have a liturgical background often find written prayers off-putting, for there is surely no adequate substitute for spontaneous prayer uttered in the Spirit? But if such a spontaneous prayer were also written down and printed, like those of Martyn Lloyd-Jones or David Yonggi Cho, could they not continue to be a blessing? So too with a written prayer that is borne out of intimacy with God. I myself never felt attracted to read written prayer devotionally until one day in deep discouragement I found myself reading a prayer of Archbishop Cranmer. What amazed me was how timely it was, and how relevant to my own situation that day. It made me see how God uses written prayers.

Much the same thing can be said of hymns. Some people feel that only the psalms should be sung since they alone are inspired. Likewise, it could be said that we should pray only the prayers in the Bible, as in John 17 or Ephesians 3:14–21. Yet when Isaac Watts broke the mould in his day and began writing his own hymns, a new era followed for which most Christians thank God. So also can prayers of God's people – ancient and modern – feed and inspire us. Years ago I was helped by a comment of John Newton (author of 'Amazing Grace') which affirmed reading written prayers in family Quiet Times when one lacked the courage or experience to pray extemporaneously before others.

We have chosen not only what we believe to be some of the better prayers of Christians living and dead; we have also sought to cross denominational and theological lines.

If the Apostle Paul could say that he was a debtor to a wide variety of people (Rom. 1:14), so can all of us surely learn from those who come from opposite traditions and cultures to our own. If we don't meet with certain people here below, we will certainly do so at the Throne of Grace! It does not follow, however, that we are in agreement with the theology of all those represented in this book. Augustus Toplady may have got off his death-bed to fight a rumour that he and John Wesley had come to terms, but both of them are worshipping together in heaven as you read these lines.

These prayers are provided so that you can use them devotionally day by day; hence the reason for following the calendar and having at least one prayer for every day of the year. We hope they do inspire you as they have blessed us; that you too might find them timely and relevant in your day-to-day life. Our prayer is that God will be more real to you than ever and that the presence of Jesus Christ will be consciously experienced by every reader. As you read and pray your way through the following pages, please remember these words from Graham Kendrick:

To keep your lovely face
Ever before my eyes,
This is my prayer,
Make it my strong desire;
That in my secret heart
No other love competes,
No rival throne survives,
And I serve only You.

R. T. KENDALL

1 January

O God, I am a sinner; I am sorry for my sin; I am willing to turn from my sin. I receive Christ as Saviour; I confess Him as Lord; I want to follow Him, and serve Him, in the fellowship of His Church. In Christ's Name. Amen.

BILLY GRAHAM

Eternal God, I place myself into your hands this coming year. May we walk together, hand in hand, and in my actions may your will be done. Amen.

GEORGE CAREY

2 January

My Lord and Saviour, I recall
when first I heard your voice,
your knock;
and opened that shut door to take you at your word.
As the years pass I ask myself
– and I ask you to show me –
whether my fellowship has deepened, my love matured,
or whether I have indeed
grown cold – a burnt-out fire?

One thing I know:
your love remains the same.
Make it then, if there is no other way,
a chastening love leading towards repentance,
rekindling love in me.

What a lot of words, Lord Jesus,
for a simple prayer!
Be Master of my house,
its hearth and warmth,
its light and sun,
its feast and comfort,
its purpose and its joy:
for your Name's sake. Amen.

TIMOTHY DUDLEY-SMITH

3 January

Late have I loved Thee, O Thou Eternal Truth and
Goodness; late have I sought Thee, my Father! But Thou
didst seek me, and when Thou shinedst forth upon me, then
I knew Thee and learnt to love Thee. I thank Thee, O my
Light, that Thou didst thus shine upon me; that Thou didst
teach my soul what Thou wouldst be to me, and didst
incline Thy face in pity unto me; Thou, Lord, hast become
my Hope, my Comfort, my Strength, my All. In Thee doth
my soul rejoice. The darkness vanished from before mine
eyes, and I beheld Thee, the Sun of Righteousness. When I
loved darkness, I knew Thee not, but wandered on from
night to night. But Thou didst lead me out of that blindness; Thou didst take me by the hand and call me to Thee,
and now I can thank Thee, and Thy mighty voice which
hath penetrated to my inmost heart. Amen.

ST AUGUSTINE

4 January

O My Lord, in thine arms I am safe; keep me and I have nothing to fear; give me up, and I have nothing to hope for. I know nothing about the future, but I rely upon Thee. I pray Thee to give me what is good for me; I pray Thee to take from me whatever may imperil my salvation. I leave it all to Thee, because Thou knowest and I do not. If thou bringest pain or sorrow on me, give me grace to bear it well, keep me from fretfulness and selfishness. If Thou givest me health and strength and success in this world, keep me ever on my guard lest these great gifts carry me away from Thee. Give me to know Thee, to believe on Thee, to love Thee, to serve Thee, to live to and for Thee. Give me to die just at that time and in that way which is most for Thy glory. Amen.

JOHN HENRY NEWMAN

5 January

Be not weary of me, good Lord, and let me not be weary of myself, or of trying to conquer myself. I am all weakness. But Thou art almighty, and can put forth Thy strength perfectly in my weakness. Make me truly to hate all which you hate, fervently to love all which you love; make me truly sorry, for love of you, that I have so often offended you, and so mightily transform me, through your grace, that I may no more offend you; through Jesus Christ. Amen.

E. B. PUSEY

6 January

Inspired by Ephesians 1:3–18

All glorious God, we give you thanks;
in your Son Jesus Christ you have given us every
    spiritual blessing in the heavenly realms.
You chose us, before the world was made,
    to be your holy people, without fault in your
    sight.
You adopted us as your children in Christ.
You have set us free by his blood,
    you have forgiven our sins.
You have made known to us your secret purpose,
    to bring heaven and earth into unity in Christ.
You have given us your Holy Spirit,
    the seal and pledge of our inheritance.
All praise and glory be yours, O God,
    for the richness of your grace,
    for the splendour of your gifts,
    for the wonder of your love.

DESMOND TUTU

7 January

Lord Jesus, help me to see what it really means to have you living in me. You feel through my emotions, hurt in my body; these things that they do to me, they do to you too. You say, 'The insults that are hurled at you have fallen on me.' Lord, when they smash my life, they smash your life too. When they insult me, they insult you in me. When they steal my reputation and good name, they steal your honour too. I know you feel angry for me and will fight on my behalf. Help me to rest in that fact. They rejected you, insulted and humiliated you as well, as they hit you over and over again. Yet you still forgave. Oh Jesus, forgive me for not forgiving too – help me love my enemy as you loved yours.

JENNIFER REES LARCOMBE

8 January

Behold, O Lord,
    I cast all my cares on you,
that I may live
    and see wondrous things out of your Law.
You know my incompetence and my infirmities;
    teach me and heal me.
Your only Son,
    he in whom are hid all the treasures of wisdom and
        knowledge,
has redeemed me with his blood.

ST AUGUSTINE

Goodness is stronger than evil;
Love is stronger than hate;
Light is stronger than darkness;
Life is stronger than death;
Victory is ours through Him who loves us.

DESMOND TUTU

9 January

O Lord our God, great, eternal, wonderful in glory, Who keepest covenant and promise for those that love Thee with their whole heart, Who art the life of all, the help of those that flee unto Thee, the hope of those who cry unto Thee cleanse us from our sins, and from every thought displeasing to Thy goodness, cleanse our souls and bodies, our hearts and consciences that with a pure heart and a clear mind, with perfect love and calm hope, we may venture confidently and fearlessly to pray unto Thee, through Jesus Christ our Lord. Amen.

ST BASIL

10 January

Prayer used in the Senate, 10 March 1948

O God our Father, let us not be content to wait and see what will happen, but give us the determination to make the right things happen.

While time is running out, save us from patience which is akin to cowardice.

Give us the courage to be either hot or cold, to stand for something, lest we fall for anything. In Jesus' name, Amen.

PETER MARSHALL

Well, Father, you know and I know I can't do anything – so show me what you are doing and draw me into that.

JOHN WIMBER

11 January

O Almighty God, who in Thy mercy hast not only delivered unto us a rule of godly living, but hast revealed Thyself in the Lord Jesus Christ, as our Father, with intent to write Thy law in our hearts; let us not, by our ingratitude or sloth, cast away this inestimable blessing; but may we offer ourselves unto Thee, our souls and bodies, to be a reasonable, true, and lively sacrifice, through Jesus Christ our Lord.

Take from us all hardness of heart; save us from all hypocrisy and feigned service. May we give up ourselves wholly unto Thee, and seek to profit more and more by the knowledge of Thy heavenly doctrine, till at the end we attain unto the fullness of Thy light. Through Jesus Christ our Lord. Amen.

JOHN CALVIN

12 January

Heavenly Father, you have told us through your Son Jesus Christ that we ought always to pray and not to faint; teach us to pray. Our spirit is willing but our flesh is weak. Give us grace each day to approach your throne and seek your face; to be concerned as much for your glory as for our need; and in everything by prayer and supplication with thanksgiving to make our requests known to you, until all our lives are gathered up into your presence and every breath is prayer, through Jesus Christ your Son, our ransom and mediator.

JOHN STOTT

13 January

Keep us from sin: give us the rule over our own spirits; and keep us from speaking unadvisedly with our lips. May we live together in peace and holy love, and do Thou command Thy blessing upon us, even life for evermore. Make us conscientious in all our dealings, always watchful against sin; as becomes those who see Thine eye ever upon them. Prepare us for all the events of the day; for we know not what a day may bring forth. Give us grace to deny ourselves; to take up our cross daily, and to follow in the steps of our Lord and Master.

We humbly pray Thee, for Christ's sake, to pardon our sins, accept our services, and grant an answer of peace to our prayers; even for His sake who died for us and rose again.

MATTHEW HENRY

14 January

And now, Lord, what is my hope?

Truly, my hope is even in Thee. Though I walk through the valley of the shadow of death, yet I will fear no evil. Lord, Thou knowest whereof we be made; Thou rememberest that we are but dust. I am Thine. Oh, save me! Behold, O Lord, that I am Thy servant, and the son of Thine handmaid. Thine unprofitable servant; yet Thy servant. Thy lost prodigal child, yet Thy child. Into Thy hands I commend myself as unto a faithful Creator. Lord, I am created in Thine own image. Suffer not Thine own image to be utterly defaced, but renew it again in righteousness and true holiness. Into Thine hands I commend myself, for Thou has redeemed me, Thou God of Truth. Amen.

LANCELOT ANDREWES

15 January

O merciful God, fill our hearts, we pray Thee, with the graces of Thy Holy Spirit – with love, joy, peace, long-suffering, gentleness, goodness, faith, meekness, temperance. Teach us to love those who hate us; to pray for those who despitefully use us; that we may be children of Thee, our Father, who makest Thy sun to shine on the evil and on the good, and sendest rain on the just and on the unjust.

In adversity, grant us grace to be patient; in prosperity, keep us humble; may we guard the door of our lips; may we lightly esteem the pleasures of the world, and thirst after heavenly things.

ANSELM

16 January

O Lord we would delight ourselves in Thee this day. Give us faith and love and hope that with these three graces we may draw very near to the Triune God. Thou wilt keep us. Thou wilt preserve us, Thou wilt feed us, Thou wilt lead us, and Thou wilt bring us to the mind of God, and there wilt Thou show us Thy love, and in the glory everlasting and boundless, there wilt Thou make us know and taste and feel the joys that cannot be expressed.

But a little longer waiting and we shall come to the golden shore; but a little longer fighting and we shall receive the crown of life that fadeth not away.

C. H. SPURGEON

17 January

Still, still with Thee, when purple morning breaketh,
  When the bird waketh, and the shadows flee;
Fairer than morning, lovelier than daylight,
  Dawns the sweet consciousness, I am with Thee.

Still, still with Thee! As to each newborn morning
  A fresh and solemn splendour still is given;
So does this blessed consciousness, awaking,
  Breathe each day nearness unto Thee and heaven.

When sinks the soul, subdued by toil to slumber,
  Its closing eye looks up to Thee in prayer;
Sweet the repose beneath Thy wings o'ershading,
  But sweeter still, to wake and find Thee there.

So shall it be at last, in that bright morning,
  When the soul waketh, and life's shadows flee;
O in that hour, fairer than daylight dawning,
  Shall rise the glorious thought – I am with Thee!

HARRIET BEECHER STOWE

18 January

O Lord, grant me to greet the coming day in peace. Help me in all things to rely upon Thy holy will. In every hour of the day reveal Thy will to me. Bless my dealings with all who surround me. Teach me to treat all that comes to me throughout the day with peace of soul, and with firm conviction that Thy will governs all. In all my deeds and words guide my thoughts and feelings. In unforeseen events let me not forget that all are sent by Thee. Teach me to act firmly and wisely, without embittering and embarrassing others. Give me strength to bear the fatigue of the coming day with all that it shall bring. Direct my will, teach me to pray, pray Thou Thyself in me. Amen.

PHILARAT

19 January

O God, You who are peace everlasting, who have taught us that the peacemakers are Your children, and whose chosen reward is the gift of peace, pour Your sweet peace into our souls, so that everything discordant may utterly vanish, and all that makes for peace be sweet to us forever.

O God, the Life of the faithful, the Bliss of the righteous, mercifully receive the prayers of Your children, so that the souls that thirst for Your promises may evermore be filled from Your abundance. Amen.

GELASIAN SACRAMENTARY

20 January

O Lord, if only my will may remain right and firm towards you, do with me whatever will please You. For it cannot be anything but good, whatever You will do with me. If it is Your will I should be in darkness, may You be blessed. If it is Your will I should be in light, may You again be blessed. If You deign to comfort me, may You be blessed. If You will have me afflicted, may You be equally blessed. O Lord, for Your sake I will cheerfully suffer whatever will come on me with Your permission.

THOMAS À KEMPIS

21 January

Father, I am aware that I can only see myself as I really am in Your light. I look at the sins of others with open eyes but often I am blind to my own weaknesses. Help me to be honest with myself.

O God, help me be more like Jesus. Give me a steadfast will and an unbroken purpose of heart that refuses to conform to what is wrong. Help me catch the quiet courage that was so evident in Your Son.

Lead me away from my petty self to Your plentiful self. I am so thankful there is a door which leads to You. Help me walk through that door, and be more concerned about others than I am about myself.

Father, I would be a person committed to You and to caring for others. And help me be faithful in the small things so that I am eligible for bigger things. Build into my life good and godly principles, I pray. In Jesus' Name. Amen.

SELWYN HUGHES

22 January

Gracious God, remember us, we beseech Thee, in our work this day. If it be Thy will, give unto us a prosperous day. May all our work be well done. May we turn nothing out half done. May we glorify Thee by honest good work; for the sake of Him Who completed His work for us, even Jesus Christ our Lord. Amen.

J. H. JOWETT

O God, may we ever seek what is true, see what is beautiful, love what is pure, and follow what is right; for the sake of Him who is Truth and Loveliness, Purity and Righteousness, even Jesus Christ our Lord. Amen.

SCRIPTURE UNION PRAYERS FOR SCHOOLS,
YOUTH GROUPS, CHURCH SERVICES AND
PERSONAL USE

23 January

Thank You, Father, for Your love. Thank You for hearing our prayers and giving us that which You know is best for us.

We thank You that we need never walk in darkness, because You are leading us and showing us the way, step by step.

Teach us, Lord, to be obedient, as You were obedient. Show us in what way we still hold on to our own will and desires, and give us the courage to leave all in Your hands.

Thank You, Father, that You will always speak to us when we come to You with a heart which is willing to hear and willing to do as You say.

CORRIE TEN BOOM

24 January

Lord, I do not know what I ought to ask of You. You only know what we need. You love me better than I know how to love myself. O Father, give to Your child that for which he himself does not know how to ask. I dare not ask either for crosses or consolations. I simply present myself before You. I open my heart to You. Behold my needs that I do not know myself. See, and do according to Your tender mercy. Smite or heal. Depress me or raise me up. I adore all Your purposes without knowing them. I am silent. I offer myself in sacrifice. I yield myself to You. I would have no other desire than to accomplish Your will. Teach me to pray. Pray Yourself in me.

FRANÇOIS DE SALIGNAC DE LA MOTHE FÉNELON

25 January

Almighty and Holy Spirit, the Comforter, pure, living, true
– illuminate, govern, sanctify me, and confirm my heart
and mind in the faith, and in all genuine consolation;
preserve and rule over me that, dwelling in the house of the
Lord all the days of my life, to behold the beauty of the
Lord, I may be and remain forever in the temple of the
Lord, and praise Him with a joyful spirit, and in union with
all the heavenly Church. Amen.

PHILIP MELANCTHON

Amen. Blessing, and glory, and wisdom, and thanksgiving,
and honour, and power, and might, be unto our God for
ever and ever. Amen.

THOMAS TORRANCE

26 January

O God, the Father of the forsaken, the help of the weak, the supplier of the needy, you teach us that love towards the race of man is the bond of perfectness and the imitation of your blessed self.

Open and touch our hearts that we may see and do, both for this world and that which is to come, the things that belong to our peace. Strengthen us in the work which we have undertaken; give us wisdom, perseverance, faith and zeal and in your own time and according to your pleasure prosper the issues, for the love of your Son, Jesus Christ.

LORD SHAFTESBURY

27 January

O Lord God, when You give Your servants
    to endeavour any great matter,
Grant us also to know that it is not the beginning,
    But the continuing of the same,
    Until it be thoroughly finished,
    Which yields the true glory.

FRANCIS DRAKE

O Lord, support us in patient thankfulness under pain,
anxiety, or loss, and move us with pity and tenderness for
our afflicted neighbours. Amen.

CHRISTINA ROSSETTI

28 January

Almighty God, Father of all mercies, we Thine unworthy servants do give Thee most humble and hearty thanks for all Thy goodness and loving kindness to us and to all men. We bless Thee for our creation, preservation, and all the blessings of this life; but above all for Thine inestimable love in the redemption of the world by our Lord Jesus Christ; for the means of grace, and for the hope of glory. And, we beseech Thee, give us that due sense of all Thy mercies, that our hearts may be unfeignedly thankful, and that we shew forth Thy praise, not only with our lips but in our lives; by giving up ourselves to Thy service, and by walking before Thee in holiness and righteousness all our days: through Jesus Christ our Lord, to whom with Thee and the Holy Ghost be all honour and glory, world without end. Amen.

BISHOP REYNOLDS OF NORWICH

29 January

Eternal Purity! Thou art brighter than the sun, purer than the angels, and the heavens are not clean in Thy sight; with mercy behold Thy servant, apt to be tempted with every object, and to be overcome by every enemy. I cannot, O God, stand in the day of battle and danger, unless Thou coverest me with Thy shield, and hidest me under Thy wings. Thou didst make me after Thine image; be pleased to preserve me so pure and spotless, that my body may be a holy temple, and my soul a sanctuary to entertain Thy divinest Spirit, the Spirit of love and holiness. Amen.

JEREMY TAYLOR

30 January

O Lord, our God, it is through Thy inconceivable greatness that we may thus call upon Thee: Lord, *our* God, *our* Creator, *our* Father, *our* Saviour; that Thou dost know and love us all, and dost desire to be known and loved by us all; that the paths of us all are seen and ruled by Thee; that we all may come before Thee, and may go to Thee.

And now we pour out all before *Thee*: our cares, that *Thou* mayest care for us; our fear, that *Thou* mayest still it; our hopes and wishes, that they may be granted not according to our will, but according to *Thy* good will; our sins, that *Thou* mayest forgive them; our thoughts and desires, that *Thou* mayest cleanse them; our whole life in this time, that *Thou* mayest lead it to the resurrection of all flesh and to eternal life, through Jesus Christ, our Lord. Amen.

KARL BARTH

31 January

Almighty God, Who art the Giver of all wisdom; enlighten our understanding with knowledge of right, and govern our wills by Thy laws, that no deceit may mislead us, nor temptation corrupt us; that we may always endeavour to do good, and to hinder evil. Amidst all the hopes and fears of this world, take not Thy Holy Spirit from us; but grant that our thoughts may be fixed on Thee, and that we may finally attain everlasting happiness, for Jesus Christ's sake. Amen.

BOOK OF CONGREGATIONAL PRAYER, 1920

O Father, my hope:
O Son, my refuge:
O Holy Spirit, my protection:
Holy Trinity, glory to thee.

ST IOANNIKOS

1 February

O Lord, who art the light, the way, the truth, the life; in whom there is no darkness, error, vanity, or death: the light without which there is darkness; the way without which there is wandering; the truth without which there is error; the life without which there is death: say, Lord, Let there be light, and I shall see light and eschew darkness; I shall see the way and avoid wandering; I shall see the truth and shun error; I shall see life, and escape death.

ST AUGUSTINE

Lord, help me to grow up before I grow old!

JOHN WIMBER

2 February

Heavenly Father, we beseech Thee, pour upon us Thine Holy Spirit, and make us in our hearts clearly to see, and steadfastly to believe, Thy gracious goodness, set forth unto us by Thine own Son, our Saviour, Jesus Christ; and make us to put all our confidence and hope of salvation in Him, whom Thou hast appointed to be our only Saviour and Redeemer. Teach us always to render unto Thee most humble and hearty thanks for Thy wondrous mercy and goodness towards us. Make us to profess the death of Thy dearly-beloved Son, in renouncing and forsaking all sin; and to rise with Him to newness of life, in righteousness and true holiness; so that after this life we may reign with Him in everlasting glory.

THOMAS CRANMER

3 February

Thanks be to Thee, my
Lord Jesus Christ,
For all the benefits which
Thou hast given me,
For all the pains and insults
which Thou has borne for me,
O most merciful Redeemer,
Friend, and Brother.
May I know Thee more clearly,
Love Thee more dearly,
And follow Thee more nearly.
Amen.

SIR RICHARD OF CHICHESTER

4 February

Our Father God, whose purpose it is to unite all things in Christ, we pray for the breaking down of barriers of misunderstanding between people of different races and colour, between employers and those who are employed, between the older and those who are young, between the successful and those who feel they have failed, between those who belong to the Church and those who remain outside. May the Spirit of Thy Son Jesus Christ, in bringing men to Thee, bring them closer to one another. We ask it for His sake. Amen.

SCRIPTURE UNION PRAYERS FOR SCHOOLS,
YOUTH GROUPS, CHURCH SERVICES AND
PERSONAL USE

5 February

O God, help us truly to want Thee. May our sincerest desire be to be like Christ. May He dominate our wills, inspire our thoughts and permeate our feelings. Help us at last to dethrone self. Kill this hateful selfishness and egotism. Deliver us from a 'humility' that parades itself for men's admiration; from doing loving things for others but with a self-congratulation that poisons motive. O God, may we be truly ready to be overlooked and forgotten and even scorned, if only Thou art glorified. Dear Christ, forgive our self-assertion and help us *really* and *truly* to want – more than anything – to be like Thee. Amen.

LESLIE WEATHERHEAD

6 February

O most merciful and gracious Father, we offer unto Thee our heartfelt thanks for Thy mercies – mercies most abundant, and undeserved ... For food and raiment and every blessing of this life we give Thee thanks. But much more for spiritual gifts, and spiritual mercies; for our new creation in Christ Jesus; for the comfort and aid of Thy Holy Spirit; for all good thoughts and desires, for all blessed means of grace ... for Thy holy word ... for the privilege of drawing nigh to Thee in prayer; above all for the priceless sacrifice of a Saviour's precious blood. We bless Thee, we praise Thee, we worship thee, ... O Lord, make us more thankful to Thee for so great and undeserved mercies, and make us more worthy of them, through Jesus Christ our Lord. Amen.

WALSHAM HOW

7 February

Almighty Father, I pray for an increasing interest in the Bible. Thou art there revealed, and there Thy will for me is made manifest. Create within me a love for thy word, and make me increasingly anxious to do all that is there commanded. Teach me to see its real and inner meaning. Open my eyes that the Bible may be a new source of joy, and strength, and guidance to my poor, sin-stained soul. Give me ears to hear Thy voice speaking as I read again the old and familiar words.

I would that this book had been my guide from the first, but I neglected its teachings, ignored its warnings, and am humiliated as I think of my treatment of it, and Thee.

WALTER JAMES

8 February

Lord and Father,
King and God,
fountain of life and immortality,
treasure of everlasting goods,
Whom the heavens hymn,
and the heaven of heavens,
the Angels and all the heavenly powers,
one to other crying continually –
and we the while, weak and unworthy,
under their feet –
Holy, Holy, Holy
Lord the God of Hosts;
full is the whole heaven,
and the whole earth,
of the majesty of Thy glory.
Blessed be the glory of the Lord
out of His place,
for His Godhead, His mysteriousness,
His height, His sovereignty, His almightiness,
His eternity, His providence.
The Lord is my strength, my stony rock, and my defence,
my deliverer, my succour, my buckler,
the horn also of my salvation and my refuge.

LANCELOT ANDREWES

9 February

If there are tracts of my life into which Christ is not allowed to come; O Lord, forgive, and help me to know more exactly what is Christ's will for me and to yield myself afresh to Him.

LESLIE WEATHERHEAD

O Lord Jesus Christ,

Draw us to thyself with the magnet of Thy mighty love, that with all our strength we may both love Thee and all for whom Thou didst die.

O Saviour of the World, who by Thy Cross and precious blood hast redeemed us, save us, and help us, we humbly beseech Thee, O Lord. Amen.

SCRIPTURE UNION PRAYERS FOR SCHOOLS,
YOUTH GROUPS, CHURCH SERVICES AND
PERSONAL USE

10 February

We offer our thanks to thee
    for sending thy only Son to die for us all.
In a world divided by colour bars,
    how sweet a thing it is to know
    that in thee we all belong to one family.

There are times when we,
      unprivileged people,
    weep tears that are not loud but deep,
    when we think of the suffering we experience.
We come to thee, our only hope and refuge.
Help us, O God, to refuse to be embittered
    against those who handle us with harshness.
      We are grateful to thee
    for the gift of laughter at all times.
Save us from hatred of those who oppress us.
May we follow the spirit of thy Son Jesus Christ.

A PRAYER FROM THE BANTU TRIBE
OF SOUTH AFRICA

11 February

Praise the Lord, O my soul: while I live will I praise the Lord; as long as I have my being, I will sing praises unto my God.

I called upon the Lord in my trouble, and the Lord heard me at large; therefore will I praise Him.

Thou art my God, and I will thank Thee; Thou are the Lord, and I will praise Thee.

'Praised be the Lord, Who hath not cast out my prayer, nor turned His mercy from me.'

'O give thanks unto the Lord, for He is gracious, and His mercy endureth for ever.'

I will not only praise Thee in secret, O Lord, but I will tell abroad what Thou hast done for my soul. I will give thanks unto Thee in the great congregation: I will praise Thee among much people.

Accept, O my God, this my sacrifice of praise and thanksgiving.

THOMAS KEN

12 February

O Jesus, my feet are dirty. Come even as a slave to me, pour water into your bowl, come and wash my feet. In asking such a thing I know I am overbold but I dread what was threatened when you said to me, 'If I do not wash your feet I have no fellowship with you.' Wash my feet then, because I long for your companionship. And yet, what am I asking? It was well for Peter to ask you to wash his feet; for him that was all that was needed for him to be clean in every part. With me it is different; though you wash me now I shall still stand in need of that other washing, the cleansing you promised when you said, 'There is a baptism I must needs be baptised with.'

ORIGEN

13 February

If Thou enlighten us not, we shall run into error; if Thou prevent not, we shall sink into sin; if Thou preserve not, we shall fall into danger. Let Thy good providence be our defence and security, and Thy Holy Spirit our comforter, guide, and counsellor, in all our ways, until through the merits of Thy son, and the multitude of Thy mercies, we are received into Thine everlasting kingdom. Grant these petitions, we beseech Thee, O Father, for the sake of Jesus Christ our Lord. Amen.

AUGUSTUS TOPLADY

Lord, make us, we implore Thee, so to love Thee that Thou mayest be to us a Fire of Love, purifying and not destroying. Amen.

CHRISTINA ROSSETTI

14 February

Glory to God in the highest,
    and on earth peace,
    goodwill among people.
We praise you, we sing to you,
we bless you, we glorify you,
we worship you,
    through the Great High Priest,
You, the One unbegotten God,
the only unapproachable being.

For your great glory,
O Lord and heavenly King,
O Lord the Father Almighty,
O Lord God,
the Father of Christ, the spotless Lamb,
which takes away the sin of the world –
you that sit upon the Cherubim,
have mercy on us and hear our prayer.

For you only are holy,
you only are the Lord Jesus Christ;
the God of all created nature,
our King,
through whom be glory, honour,
and worship to you.

APOSTOLIC CONSTITUTIONS

15 February

O Lord our God, grant us grace to desire Thee with our whole heart; that, so desiring, we may seek and find Thee; and so finding Thee, may love Thee; and loving Thee, may hate those sins, from which Thou hast redeemed us.

Grant unto us, we pray Thee, repentant hearts, contrite spirits; eyes that can weep for sin; hands that can help the needy. Quench in us, O thou Lord of our life, all sinful desires; and kindle, instead thereof, the fire of holy love. O our Redeemer, take from us the spirit of pride, and enrich us with the treasure of Thy humility. Cleanse our hearts from the evil passions of anger, malice, envy, and all uncharitableness; and make us patient, kind, and tender-hearted. Grant unto us a perfect faith, a sure hope, and a love that never faileth.

ANSELM

16 February

Our Father, who art in heaven, hallowed be thy name:
To sing the praise of God, it is that for which we were
made, and it is that which will be, for all eternity, our greatest joy.

    Thy kingdom come:
The gospel values of Jesus – justice, love and peace –
embraced throughout the whole world and in all their
fullness.

    Thy will be done on earth as it is in heaven:
That's the only thing, which really matters; what you want
for us is best for us.

Father, into your hands I commend my spirit.

'It is your face, O Lord, that I seek.
Hide not your face.'

BASIL HUME

17 February

O God, I asked for strength that I might achieve; I was made weak that I might learn humbly to obey. I asked for help that I might do greater things; I was given infirmity that I might do better things. I asked for riches that I might be happy; I was given poverty that I might be wise. I asked for power that I might have the praise of men: I was given weakness that I might feel the need of God. I asked for all things that I might enjoy life; I was given life that I might enjoy all things. I got nothing that I asked for but everything I hoped for. Almost despite myself, my unspoken prayers were answered. I am among all men most richly blessed.

A CONFEDERATE SOLDIER

18 February

Fill us, we pray Thee, with Thy light and life, that we may show forth Thy wondrous glory. Grant that Thy love may so fill our lives that we may count nothing too small to do for Thee, nothing too much to give, and nothing too hard to bear. So teach us, Lord, to serve Thee as Thou deservest, to give and not to count the cost, to fight and not to heed the wounds, to toil and not to seek for rest, to labour and not to ask for any reward save that of knowing that we do Thy will. Amen.

IGNATIUS OF LOYOLA

19 February

So fill us with Thy Spirit, O Lord, that we, passing from one thing to another, may go from strength to strength, everywhere full of Thy praise, everywhere full of Thy work, finding the joy of the Lord to be our strength, until the time when the work of this world shall close, and the weary hours shall come to an end, and darkness shall come, and our eyes shall rest for a while, then give us an abundant entrance into life eternal; through Jesus Christ our Lord. Amen.

GEORGE DAWSON

Hide us, we entreat Thee, in Thine own Presence from the provoking of all men. By Thy holy love and fear, keep us from sins of temper and of the tongue. Amen.

CHRISTINA ROSSETTI

20 February

I am no longer my own but Yours.
Put me to what you will.
Put me to doing. Put me to suffering.
Let me be employed for You, or laid aside for You,
Exalted for You, or brought low for You.
Let me be full, let me be empty.
Let me have all things, let me have nothing.
I freely and wholeheartedly yield all things to
Your pleasure and disposal.
And now glorious and blessed God,
Father, Son and Holy Spirit,
You are mine and I am Yours. So be it.
And this covenant now made on earth,
Let it be satisfied in Heaven. Amen.

JOHN WESLEY

21 February

O Lord, Who hast 'loved us with an everlasting love', teach us to love Thee with undivided hearts.

O Lord Jesus Christ, Who hast said: 'A new commandment I give unto you, that ye love one another as I have loved you', teach us the greatness of Thy love. Inspire us to love one another as Thou hast loved us; Teach us to bear one another's burdens; and to seek one another's good.

Grant, O Lord, that the love of God may be shed abroad in our hearts by the Holy Ghost given unto us. Grant us ever to abide in Thy Love. And to Thee, O Father, Son, and Holy Ghost be all honour and glory, now and evermore. Amen.

THOMAS HALL

22 February

O most Glorious God, in Jesus Christ my merciful and loving Father, I acknowledge and confess my guilt, in the weak and imperfect performance of the duties of this day. I have called on Thee for pardon and forgiveness of sins, but so coldly and carelessly, that my prayers are become my sin and stand in need of pardon.

GEORGE WASHINGTON

Grant us, O Lord, we beseech You, always to seek Your kingdom and righteousness. And of whatever You see us to stand in need, mercifully grant us an abundant portion. Amen.

MARY TILESTON

23 February

Heavenly Father, you have blessed our weekday work both by your own work of creation and by your Son's labour at a carpenter's bench. Enable those of us with work to do, not only to find fulfilment in it ourselves, but also to enjoy the privilege of cooperating with you in the service of the community, through Jesus Christ our Lord.

JOHN STOTT

O Our Father, may the influence and presence of Thy Holy Spirit abide with us today. May every week be as a long sabbath of unbroken holiness. May every task be sanctified; for the sake of Jesus Christ our Lord and Saviour. Amen.

J. H. JOWETT

24 February

O Holy Spirit, Love of God, powerful Advocate and sweetest Comforter, infuse Your grace and descend plentifully into my heart, for in whom You dwell the Father and the Son come likewise and inhabit that breast. O come, Thou Cleanser of all inward pollutions, and Healer of spiritual wounds and diseases. Come, in much mercy, and make me fit to receive You.

ST AUGUSTINE

Jesus, see me at Thy feet,
    Nothing but Thy Blood can save me;
Thou alone my need canst meet,
    Nothing but Thy Blood can save me.

RICHARD SLATER

25 February

Oh blessed Lord! How much I need
Thy Light to guide me on my way!
So many hands, that, without heed,
Still touch Thy wounds and make them bleed,
So many feet that day by day
Still wander from Thy fold astray!
Feeble at best is my endeavour!
I see but cannot reach the height
That lies for ever in the Light;
And yet for ever and for ever,
When seeming just within my grasp,
I feel my feeble hands unclasp,
And sink discouraged into night –
For Thine own purpose Thou has sent
The strife and the discouragement.

HENRY WADSWORTH LONGFELLOW

26 February

Lord, what can I say? I am Thine. Keep me simply Thine. To body, soul and spirit come with an influx of life. Lord, through all the multitudinous duties of the day keep me calm, ennoble by Thy touch and tenderness. O Lord, it is Thee I want, strong and mighty and pure. Settle me and quieten me down in Thee. Thy word says, 'Casting all your cares upon Him, for He careth for you.' What a wonder those words are! Lord, I look to Thee that I may be renewed in the spirit of my mind.

How entirely I look to Thee! Unto Thee do I come in great and glad expectancy. Cleanse me from flurry, and keep me purely and calmly Thine. Gather me into concentrated peace in Thee.

OSWALD CHAMBERS

27 February

Lord, we pray to you, knowing you watch over us. You not only created our souls and made our bodies, you are the Saviour, Ruler and Guide of all people. You love us so much that you give us reconciliation and peace.

Be kind to us, Lord; help and heal those who are ill, cure their diseases; and raise up those who are depressed. We glorify your holy Name through Jesus Christ, your only Son. By him may power and glory be yours, in the Holy Spirit, now and age after age. Amen.

SERAPION OF THMUIS EUCHOLOGIUM

28 February

Eternal God, fountain of all love, trusting in your love I come before you, to speak to you, to ask you for your love. You know all I would ask you if I dared; you know how I would love you if I could; you know all I would hope for in you, if my own unworthiness did not keep me back. Yet you give me the longing, you will give what I long for, even yourself, whom I long for. You prepare the heart. Prepare my heart, O loving God, that I may long for you more, adore you more humbly, ask at least, with all the desires of my heart, all which you are ready to give me, which you have prepared for me, if I love you. Make me love you through all your love for me, through your own love in me. Amen.

E. B. PUSEY

29 February

Jesus, our Master, do Thou walk with us while we walk in the way and long to reach the country, so that following Thy light, we may keep the way of righteousness, and never wander away into the darkness of this world's night whilst Thou Who art the Way, the Truth, and the Life art shining within us; These things we ask for Thine own Name's sake. Amen

MOZARABIC LITURGY

Grant, O Lord, that we may be saved from all pettiness and self-seeking; may be filled with a gallant and undaunted spirit, and may be diffusers of life, invigorating all we meet, through Jesus Christ our Lord. Amen.

THOMAS HALL

1 March

Almighty and ever blessed God our Heavenly Father,

Lord, hear us as thus we commit all thy people and all thy servants to thy tender care, and hear us, O Lord, as we intercede on behalf of the world in its pain and sin and shame and confusion.

God, have mercy upon the nations. We pray for those whom thou hast appointed to rule and to govern in this and in all the lands. We pray thee to humble them under thine almighty hand.

Hear us, O Lord, in these our prayers; receive again, we ask, our unworthy and humble praise as we offer it all, pleading nothing but the name and the merit of thy dear Son our Lord and Saviour Jesus Christ. Amen.

D. MARTYN LLOYD-JONES

2 March

Worthy of praise from every mouth,
    of confession from every tongue,
    of worship from every creature
Is Thy glorious Name, O Father, Son and Holy Ghost;
    Who didst create the world in Thy grace
    and by Thy compassion didst save the world.
To Thy majesty, O God, ten thousand times ten thousand
    bow down and adore,
Singing and praising without ceasing, and saying,
    Holy, holy, holy, Lord God of hosts;
Heaven and earth are full of Thy praises;
    Hosanna in the highest.

NESTORIAN LITURGY

O Lord, how great You are! I can only bow down and
worship You for Your majesty and wisdom.

CORRIE TEN BOOM

3 March

Father, You are worthy to receive glory and honour and power for from You, through You and to You are all things.

Thank You for helping me to understand that I only discover my real reason for existence as I learn to praise You through Jesus Christ, Your Son and my Saviour. I bow in wonder before Your amazing wisdom revealed in the plan of salvation, and I thank You that Your salvation has become real in my life.

Please keep on enlightening the eyes of my heart so that knowing You better I may praise You better. Help me to enjoy praising You so much that I may honestly anticipate the joys of heaven. I ask this for the praise of Your Name and in the Name of the Lord Jesus Christ. Amen.

DEREK PRIME

4 March

Almighty God, Father, Son and Holy Spirit, I lift my heart in adoration to Thee this day. Thou art my Creator, my Redeemer, my Sanctifier, my Preserver, my Provider and my All in All. The great desire of my heart is to know Thee and to make Thee known.

I confess that there is no good thing in me and that Thou lovest me not because of what I am, but in spite of all that I am. Purify me from every sin and set my heart ablaze with love for Thee. Too often my prayers have become my sin because of their coldness. Kindle within my soul a red hot passion for those who even now are on the precipice of perdition. May I be satisfied with nothing less than turning the world upside down as the Apostles did. Take the brief span of my life and use it for the advancement of the kingdom of my Lord Jesus Christ throughout this world. In His most glorious name I pray. Amen.

JAMES KENNEDY

5 March

My Saviour, it would be a sad thing for me if Thou shouldest withdraw Thyself from my life. My desire for goodness, and my sorrow for sin, are the fruits of Thy presence within me; and if Thou shouldest leave me, all chance of my ever becoming pure would vanish. I thank Thee, Jesus, my Friend Divine, for Thy presence with me every day. Live increasingly in my soul. Take entirely within Thy ruling every movement and motive of my soul. Inspire my lightest words. Give me every day an increased consciousness of Thy presence. Let it be a bright and vivid reality; not a kill-joy, but a constant inspiration, a never-ceasing source of happiness. Make it true for me to say: 'Thou, O Christ, art all I want.'

WALTER JAMES

6 March

Merciful God, whose heart beats in Jesus Christ with infinite love for all thy children, be entreated of us for all thy human children. Let the Gospel of thy grace be heard by all peoples of the earth; let the power of the Cross vanquish the pride of nations, until they bring their homage to thy throne and through judgement and mercy are made partakers of thine eternal Kingdom: in the peace of Jesus Christ our Lord.

THOMAS TORRANCE

Lord, through the Holy Spirit make me an articulate, joyful witness for You. I need to look to You, and not to myself. Turn my eyes, through the Holy Spirit, in the right direction.

CORRIE TEN BOOM

7 March

We thank Thee that we have again laid us down in peace and slept, because Thou, O Lord, hast made us to dwell in safety. Into Thy hands we commit our bodies and spirits, for our going out and coming in this day. We are more exposed by day than by night, more surrounded with evil, and more liable to the seductions of sin. May we ever regard sin as our greatest enemy, and holiness as our noblest attainment. And whether we are in solitude or society, may we derive comfort from the fact that Thou God seest us. Hear us, we beseech Thee, for Jesus Christ's sake. Amen.

FIELDING OULD

8 March

Dear Lord, may I take Thee with me today 'in my heart', do nothing that would grieve Thee, say nothing that I should be ashamed to say in Thy physical presence, think nothing that is unworthy, and go nowhere where I should be ashamed to be found by Thee. Let the thought of Thy real presence with me dominate my life today. Amen.

LESLIE WEATHERHEAD

My God, I am wholly Yours.
God of Love,
I love You with all my heart.
Lord, fashion me according to Your heart.

BROTHER LAWRENCE

9 March

O God our Father, who hast set forth the way of life for us in Thy beloved Son: we confess with shame our slowness to learn of Him, our reluctance to follow Him. Thou hast spoken and called, and we have not given heed; Thy beauty has shone forth and we have been blind; Thou hast stretched out Thy hands to us through our fellows and we have passed by. We have taken great benefits with little thanks; we have been unworthy of Thy changeless love. Have mercy upon us and forgive, O Lord.

METHODIST BOOK OF OFFICES

10 March

I know that the Immovable comes down;
I know that the Invisible appears to me;
I know that he who is far outside the whole creation
Takes me within himself and hides me in his arms,
And then I find myself outside the whole world.
I, a frail, small mortal in the world,
Behold the Creator of the world, all of him, within myself;
And I know that I shall not die, for I am within the Life,
I have the whole of Life springing up as a fountain
    within me.
He is in my heart, he is in heaven:
Both there and here he shows himself to me with
    equal glory.

ST SYMEON THE NEW THEOLOGIAN

11 March

Lord of all power and might, who are the Author and Giver of all good things, it is our blessed privilege to draw near to Thee in the name of Christ. Give us true joy in worshipping Thee. We adore and praise Thee for the daily mercies we have received through our whole lives.

O Eternal God, teach us to see more clearly the shortness of time, and the nearness of eternity. Our days and weeks pass quickly away. Our joys and sorrows are but for a moment: but Thou hast promised to Thy children an eternal weight of glory. Help us, O Father, to seek those things which are above. If any before Thee have neglected to seek Thy favour hitherto, may we seek Thee at once through Thy well-beloved Son. O draw us to Thyself, and open our eyes to see the vanity of things below.

GEORGE EVERARD

12 March

God, above whom is nothing, beyond whom is nothing, without whom is nothing. God, under whom is the whole, in whom is the whole, with whom is the whole. Who hast made man after thine image and likeness, which he discovers who has come to know himself. Hear me, hear me, graciously hear me, my God, my Lord, My King, my Father, my Cause, my Hope, my Wealth, my Honour, my House, my Country, my Health, my Light, my Life. Hear, hear, hear me graciously, in that way, all thine own, which though known to few is to those few known so well.

ST AUGUSTINE

13 March

Thou hast ordained that we should pass through this life as travellers, till Thou gatherest us to Thy heavenly rest. Give us grace to bear in mind that heavenly inheritance which Thou hast set before us. So guide us in our journey that we stray not, neither depart from the way; but keep us ever looking forward to the prize of our high calling, until we shall have finished our course with joy. May we behold by faith things invisible; and may our dependence be on Thee alone; may we so trust to Thy gracious providence as not to doubt our safety, since life and salvation are Thy care. So, when troubles or storms assault us, we shall still remain in peace, till we finally enjoy that blessed and eternal rest which Thou hast prepared for us in heaven, through Jesus Christ our Lord. Amen.

JOHN CALVIN

14 March

As I enter your holy presence, Lord,
in this quiet room
I find it hard to imagine
the great temple, the smoking sacrifice,
the lambs and kids awaiting slaughter,
the knives, the blood, the solemn ceremony
of life poured out
to take away your people's sins.

It is, I recognise, still by blood.
I come, as they came, only by sacrifice.
But my Lamb of Sacrifice is Jesus.
Upon his sacred head I lay my sins.
        O Lord, my God and Father,
If all that ritual of blood could never purge man's guilt,
but only point to Christ the Lamb of God,
how can any man be free of guilt
gnawing unnoticed in the secret places of his soul?

Only through Christ:
but perfectly through him.
He is the true and living way, the sin-bearer, and
the risen Saviour.
In him, I rest and I rejoice.

Amen.

TIMOTHY DUDLEY-SMITH

15 March

Father, you promised to hide yourself from the wise and prudent and reveal yourself to little children. When I realised one day that Jesus prayed this prayer, it opened heaven for me. It made me know that I could finally rest knowing you were watching over me.

Thank you that you take delight in revealing yourself with miraculous displays of your Spirit to those who have ingenuous trust. I don't ever want to be complex or sophisticated if it means you would hide these things from me. I want to be fascinated with your miracles and overjoyed when you answer my prayers. Lord, I ask you to help my heart to react in wonder every time I hear that you have revealed yourself to someone or touched them with your power. I want to be in awe of your presence as if every time you are near it is like the first time I knew you were there.

JOHN ARNOTT

16 March

Praised be Thou, O God, who dost make the day bright with Thy sunshine, and the night with the beams of heavenly fires. Listen now to my prayers; watch over me with Thy power; give me grace to pass all the days of my life blamelessly, free from sin and terror. For with Thee is mercy and plenteous redemption, O Lord, my God.

GREEK LITURGY

Lord, forgive what I have been, sanctify what I am; and order what I shall be. Amen.

MARY TILESTON

17 March

I bind unto myself today
The power of God to hold and lead;
His eye to watch, his might to stay,
His ear to hearken to my need;
The wisdom of my God to teach,
His hand to guide, his shield to ward,
The word of God to give me speech,
His heavenly host to be my guide.

Christ be with me, Christ within me,
Christ behind me, Christ before me,
Christ beside me, Christ to win me,
Christ to comfort and restore me,
Christ beneath me, Christ above me,
Christ in quiet, Christ in danger,
Christ in hearts of all that love me,
Christ in mouth of friend and stranger.

I bind unto myself today ...
The strong name of the Trinity.

ST PATRICK
(*His Breastplate*)

18 March

O Thou Who art the true Sun of the world, evermore rising and never going down, Who by Thy most wholesome
appearing and sight dost nourish and make joyful all things,
as well that are in heaven as also that are on earth, we
beseech Thee mercifully and favourably to shine into our
hearts, that the night and darkness of sin, and the mists of
error on every side being driven away, Thou brightly shining within our hearts, we may all our life long, go without
any stumbling or offence, and may walk as in the daytime,
being pure and clean from the works of darkness, and
abounding in all good works which Thou hast prepared for
us to walk in; through Jesus Christ our Lord. Amen.

DESIDERIUS ERASMUS

19 March

I offer up unto thee my prayers and intercessions, for those especially who have in any matter hurt, grieved, or found fault with me, or who have done me any damage or displeasure.

For all those also whom, at any time, I may have vexed, troubled, burdened, and scandalised, by words or deeds, knowingly or in ignorance; that Thou wouldst grant us all equally pardon for our sins, and for our offences against each other.

Take away from our hearts, O Lord, all suspiciousness, indignation, wrath, and contention, and whatsoever may lessen brotherly love.

O Lord, have mercy on those that crave Thy mercy, give grace unto them that stand in need thereof, and make us to enjoy Thy grace, and go forward to life eternal. Amen.

THOMAS À KEMPIS

20 March

God, heavenly Father,
The story of my life is not unlike the writing of a book.
The dawning of each day is not unlike the turning
of a fresh new page, white and clean, perfectly blank,
waiting to be filled with the actions and words of today.
I am ashamed when I think of those earlier pages,
of the volume of days that went to make up
the story of my life.
It was your Son who made the difference to my record,
by his entry into our world.
Living and dying, he wrote a new story,
my story.
Father, let me dedicate this new day to you,
in love and gratitude for all that you have done.
May I see today as the writing of a new fresh page,
the story of my life in yours
and yours in mine.

RICHARD BEWES

21 March

Show Thyself, O Lord and have pity on Thy child, and bring his steps into the way of peace. Thou that knowest our thoughts, make Thyself known to our hearts; Thou that art from everlasting, let us behold Thy truth. Hast Thou not made our souls in Thy likeness? Take away the stain from the glass, and let us behold in it Thine image. When Thou willest, Thy word goeth forth; Thou breathest forth Thy love, and our souls are joined to Thee. Take away from me shame and rebuke; renew in me Thy strength, and show me the way of peace. Turn me again, and I shall be turned; take away the darkness which hideth Thee, and in the light of the living God let me see light. Amen.

ROWLAND WILLIAMS

22 March

Thou knowest, O heavenly Father, the duties that lie before us this day, the dangers that may confront us, the sins that most beset us. Guide us, strengthen us, protect us.

Give us Thy life in such abundance that we may this day hold our souls in Thy pure light. Give us Thy power that we may become a power for righteousness among our fellows. Give us Thy love that all lesser things may have no attraction for us; that selfishness, impurity, and falsehood may drop away as dead desires, holding no meaning for us. Let us find Thy power, Thy love, Thy life in all mankind, and in the secret places of our own souls. Amen.

MABEL DEARMER

23 March

O God the Father, Who didst not spare Thy only begotten Son, but didst deliver Him up for us all; O God the Son, Who didst die upon the cross that Thou mightest put away sin by the sacrifice of Thyself; O God the Eternal Spirit, through Whom that sacrifice was offered – three Persons and one God – we adore the unspeakable greatness of redeeming love. Inasmuch as we are partakers of His death, we are called upon to take up our cross daily. Lord, enable us to deny ourselves, to spend and be spent in Thy service. Grant us grace to glorify Thy Name; through Jesus Christ our Lord. Amen.

GORDON CALTHROP

24 March

O Thou lover of mankind, bless all Thy people, the flocks of Thy fold. Send down into our hearts the peace of heaven, and grant us also the peace of this life. Give life to the souls of all of us, and let no deadly sin prevail against us, or any of Thy people. Deliver all who are in trouble, for Thou art our God, Who settest the captives free; Who givest hope to the hopeless, and help to the helpless; Who liftest up the fallen; and Who art the Haven of the ship-wrecked. Preserve us in our pilgrimage through this life from hurt and danger, and grant that we may end our lives as Christians, well-pleasing to Thee, and free from sin, and that we may have our portion and lot with all Thy saints; for the sake of Jesus Christ our Lord and Saviour. Amen.

LITURGY OF ST MARK

25 March

O Lord Jesus Christ, full of mercy and truth; have mercy upon me according to Thy great mercy.

O Jesus, who didst create me, and with Thy precious blood didst redeem me, suffer me not to be condemned, whom Thou didst make out of nothing.

Jesus, acknowledge what is Thine in me, and take away from me all that is not Thine.

O Jesus, pour into me Thy grace, wisdom, charity, chastity, and humility, and in all mine adversities, holy patience, that I may be able to love Thee perfectly, and in Thee to make my boast and to find my chief delight in Thee for ever and ever. Amen.

ST BERNARDINE

26 March

We rejoice, O Lord our God, in Thy almighty power and glory. Raise Thou us up with Thee, O blessed Saviour, above all earthly desires. Inspire us with thoughts of joy, of hope, and love. Enter Thou within the chamber of our hearts, and say unto us, 'Peace be unto you.' Give us the grace to see Thee, blessed Saviour, the eyes of our understanding being enlightened, that we may know Thee walking by our side, in this our earthly pilgrimage. Come unto us, O our Lord, and dwell within us.

ST BERNARDINE

27 March

Cleanse us, O Lord, and keep us undefiled, that we may be numbered among those blessed ones, who having washed their robes, and made them white in the Blood of the Lamb, stand before Thy throne, and praise Thee day and night in Thy temple; for Jesus Christ's sake. Amen.

JOHN HUNTER

Grant we beseech Thee, merciful Lord, to Thy faithful people pardon and peace, that they may be cleansed from all their sins, and serve Thee with a quiet mind, through Jesus Christ our Lord. Amen.

BOOK OF COMMON PRAYER

28 March

Thou art the great God – the one who is in heaven.
It is thou, thou Shield of Truth,
it is thou, thou Tower of Truth,
it is thou, thou Bush of Truth,
it is thou, thou who sittest in the highest,
thou art the creator of life.
Thou art the Hunter who hunts for souls.
Thou art the Leader who goes before us.
Thou art the Great Mantle which covers us.
Thou art he whose hands are wounded;
thou art he whose feet are wounded;
thou art he whose blood is a trickling stream – and why?
Thou art he whose blood was spilled for us.
For this great price we call,
for thine own place we call.

A PRAYER FROM THE XHOSA TRIBE
OF SOUTH AFRICA

29 March

Lord Jesus, come with me into the darkness of the cellar where I have hidden so many frightening things. I've shoved feelings down there because there wasn't time to process them – memories I couldn't face, emotions I thought were wrong and must be suppressed, fears, doubts, resentment, and yes, furious anger! Shine your light on these things I never wanted to see again, and help me remember things I would much rather forget. Handle my reactions with me, and show me how to bear the pain of it all. I am so afraid of the dark; please come with me, and one by one we can bring these things to the surface and out into your sunlight. Lord, I am ashamed that I felt as I did, and as I still do. Forgive me, heal me, help me to let it go. I give you my darkness, and in exchange I receive your light.

JENNIFER REES LARCOMBE

30 March

Father glorify Thy Son. Somehow our prayer always comes to this before we have done. 'Father glorify Thy Son that Thy Son also may glorify Thee', and let the days come when He shall see of the travail of His soul and shall be satisfied. Bless all work done for Thee, whether it be in the barn or in the cathedral, silently and quietly at the street door, or in the Sunday-school or in the classes, O Lord bless Thy work. Hear also prayers that have been put up by wives for their husbands, children for their parents, parents for their children. Let the holy service of prayer never cease, and let the intercession be accepted of God, for Jesus Christ's sake. Amen.

C. H. SPURGEON

31 March

O my God, my whole life has been a course of mercies and blessings shown to one who has been most unworthy of them. Year after year Thou hast carried me on, removed dangers from my path, refreshed me, borne with me, directed me, sustained me. O forsake me not, when my strength faileth me. And Thou never wilt forsake me. I may securely repose upon Thee. While I am true to Thee, Thou wilt still, and to the end, be superabundantly good to me. I may rest upon Thy arm; I may go to sleep in Thy bosom. Only give me, and increase in me, that true loyalty to Thee, which is the bond of the covenant between Thee and me, and the pledge in my own heart and conscience that Thou, the Supreme God, wilt not forsake me. Amen.

JOHN HENRY NEWMAN

1 April

We thank Thee for the mercies of the night past; that we laid down and slept, and waked up again in safety; because Thou hast sustained us, we are brought in safety to the beginning of another day. We acknowledge that we are cold and defective in our love to Thee; we are weak in our desires after Thee; and cannot walk with Thee as we ought to do. But we pray Thee to forgive all our sins for Christ's sake, and be at peace with us, in Him who died to make peace, and ever liveth making intercession for us. Grant us strength for all the duties of the day; that we may do all things after a godly sort, acknowledging Thee in all our ways; and be Thou pleased to direct our steps.

MATTHEW HENRY

2 April

We pray for kids on city streets –
    even when they rob us.
We pray for purity in teenagers –
    even when they seduce each other.
We pray for children who could be learning –
    even when they sit in class like zombies.
We pray for the goodness that is buried in young druggies –
    even when they are hustling people.
We pray for them all in the name of the light
    that shines in the darkness –
    because we know that darkness cannot put it out.
We pray for them all in the name of the light
    that lights everyone who comes into the world.
We pray for them all in the name of the light who
    gives us substance of things hoped for
    and is the evidence of things not seen.

TONY CAMPOLO

3 April

O Lord, long-suffering and abundant in Goodness and Truth, fill us, I beseech Thee, with graces. Make us long-suffering and patient, cordial and sympathising, kind and good; teach us to hold and speak the truth in love, and to show mercy that we also obtain mercy. Faithful Lord, grant to us, I pray Thee, faithful hearts devoted to Thee, and to the service of all men for Thy sake. Fill us with pure love of Thee, keep us steadfast in this love, give us faith that worketh by love, and preserve us faithful unto death. Amen.

CHRISTINA ROSSETTI

4 April

Blessed be Thy Name for the peace, rest, and safety of the night past. Enable us, in the strength of Thy grace and of Thy gifts, to love Thee truly, to serve Thee faithfully, and to depend on Thee without wavering. Give us grace to acknowledge Thee in all our ways, and be Thou graciously pleased to establish our goings, and to direct our paths. Grant us Thy fatherly protection, and the heavenly guidance of Thy good Spirit, to choose our inheritance for us, and to dispose of us, and all that belongs to us, to the glory of Thy great Name.

AUGUSTUS TOPLADY

5 April

O Lord, let me not henceforth desire health or life, except to spend them for Thee, with Thee, and in Thee. Thou alone knowest what is good for me; do, therefore, what seemeth Thee best. Give to me, or take from me; conform my will to Thine; and grant that, with humble and perfect submission, and in holy confidence, I may receive the orders of Thine eternal Providence; and may equally adore all that comes to me from Thee, through Jesus Christ our Lord. Amen.

BLAISE PASCAL

6 April

On your last days on earth
you promised
to leave us the Holy Spirit
as our present comforter.
We also know that your Holy Spirit blows over this earth.
But we do not understand him.
Many think
he is only wind or a feeling.
Let your Holy Spirit
break into our lives.
Let him come like blood into our veins,
so that we will be driven
entirely by your will.
Let your Spirit
blow over wealthy Europe and America,
so that men there will be humble.
Let him blow over the poor parts of the world,
so that men there need suffer no more.
Let him blow over Africa,
so that men here may understand
what true freedom is.
There are a thousand voices and spirits
in this world,
but we want to hear only your voice,
and be open only to your Spirit.

A PRAYER FROM GHANA

7 April

O Lord Jesus, sweetest guest. Blessed art Thou, O Lord, in the highest, for Thou hast come into my heart, Thou Day-spring from on High. O King of Peace! Drive from my heart all vain and idle thoughts, that my soul may be able to dwell on and to love Thee only, the author of peace.

For thou art the true peace of the heart, Thou art its only Rest, and out of Thee all is restless and unquiet.

Grant me Thy grace, most merciful Jesus, that it may be with me, and work with me, and continue with me even to the end. Grant me ever to will and to desire what is most pleasing unto Thee.

SIR HENRY S. LUNN

8 April

Lord God Almighty, Our Lord Jesus said He had all power granted unto Him; I want to draw on His grace more, and realise His power and patience and purpose in my life. Come in Thy great and quiet almightiness and speak with power today.

Lord, I do praise Thee that in Christ Jesus it is all of Thee, it is mercy and loving-kindness, graciousness and wonders all along the way. I would be sensitive to Thee and Thy doings, and Christ-like in my gratitude. Oh, to be freely and greatly taken up by Thee. How I need to realise that apart from Thee I can do nothing.

OSWALD CHAMBERS

9 April

O Heavenly Father, the Father of all wisdom, understanding, and true strength, I beseech Thee, look mercifully upon me, and send Thy Holy Spirit into my breast; that when I must join to fight in the field for the glory of Thy holy Name, then I, being strengthened with the defence of Thy right hand, may manfully stand in the confession of Thy faith, and of Thy truth, and continue in the same unto the end of my life, through our Lord Jesus Christ. Amen.

NICHOLAS RIDLEY

This only do I ask of thy extreme kindness.
That thou convert me wholly to thee
And thou allow nothing to prevent me
from wending my way to thee.

ST AUGUSTINE

10 April

The fetters thou imposest, O Lord, are wings of freedom. There is no liberty like the liberty of being bound to go.

When Thou layest upon me the sense of obligation, that moment Thou settest my spirit free. When Thou sayest that I must, my heart says, 'I can.' My strength is proportionate to the strength of those cords that bind me. I am never so unrestrained as when I am constrained by Thy love. Evermore, Thou Divine Spirit, guide me by this instinct of the right. Put round about my heart the cord of Thy captivating love, and draw me whither in my own light I would not go. Bind me to Thyself as Thou bindest the planets to the sun, that it may become the very law of my nature to be led by Thee. May I be content to know that goodness and mercy shall *follow* me without waiting to see them in advance of me. Amen.

GEORGE MATHESON

11 April

Hail, Father, source of the Son,
Son, the Father's image;
Father, the ground where the Son stands,
Son, the Father's seal;
Father, the power of the Son,
Son, the Father's beauty;
All-pure Spirit, bond between
the Father and the Son.
Send, O Christ, the Spirit,
send the Father to my soul;
Steep my dry heart in this dew,
the best of all thy gifts.

SYNESIUS OF CYRENE

Lord Jesus, thank You that You are always with me and that, when I look up, I see You. Everything else becomes small, compared to this joy.

CORRIE TEN BOOM

12 April

We thank Thee, Father, Son, and Holy Spirit, for our salvation; we thank Thee, the One God, for Thy blessings to us. May we not only feel Thee near us, but hear Thee saying, 'I have not called thee servant, but friend', and may we not shrink from the contemplation, owing to our unworthiness, but be aided by Thy Spirit, to realise and understand what it is to be Thy friends, and to know that we are the friends of Christ. By taking away sin, dry up the fountain of sorrow.

Grant unto us the spirit of intense sympathy for all sufferers. May we do our utmost to wipe away tears from off all faces.

Wherever we walk, may we walk with God.

SAMUEL MARTIN

13 April

Lord Jesus, the weaker I am in this wheelchair, the harder I lean on you. And the harder I lean on you, the stronger I discover you to be. Keep my heart strong, my soul stirred, my vision clear and my enthusiasm fresh to help others know you this way. Help me to boast in my affliction so that others might delight in theirs. Your power and peace is worth it all; and your glory, worth more. Jesus, in short, I would rather be in this chair knowing you this way, than on my feet without you. And at journey's end, may I testify, one more time, that your grace was enough. Amen.

JONI EARECKSON TADA

14 April

O Lord, the Lord whose ways are right, keep us in Thy mercy from lip-service and empty forms; from having a name that we live, but being dead. Help us to worship Thee by righteous deeds and lives of holiness; that our prayer also may be set forth in Thy sight as the incense, and the lifting up of our hands be as an evening sacrifice.

Plant in our hearts love which is the fulfilling of the law. Teach us to love Thee with our whole will and being, and our neighbour as ourselves. Keep us from dividing Thy commandments into great and small, according to our own blind estimate; but give us grace humbly to acknowledge that whoso transgresseth in one point is guilty of the whole law. Amen.

CHRISTINA ROSSETTI

15 April

O God, who knowest all our foolishness, and from whom our sins are not hid, have mercy upon us after Thy loving-kindness; and, according to the multitude of Thy tender mercies, blot out our transgressions. Forgive us all the evil we have done; condemn us not for all the good we have omitted; but, for the sake of Thy beloved Son, in whom we have redemption through His blood, receive us graciously, and love us freely.

Almighty God, who workest in us to will and to do of Thy good pleasure, give us grace that we may truly repent of all our sins, and heartily yield ourselves up to Thy service. Let it be the work of our whole lives to obey Thee – the joy of our souls to please Thee – the satisfaction of all our desires, and the fulfilment of all our hopes, to walk with Thee in the comforts of Thy fellowship, and to dwell with Thee in the glories of Thy kingdom.

PRAYERS FOR SOCIAL AND FAMILY WORSHIP
(by the Church of Scotland)

16 April

Lord, make me an instrument of Thy peace.
Where there is hatred, let me sow love;
Where there is injury, pardon;
Where there is doubt, faith;
Where there is despair, hope;
Where there is darkness, light;
Where there is sadness, joy.

O Divine Master, grant that
I may not so much seek
To be consoled, as to console;
Not so much to be understood, as to understand;
Not so much to be loved, as to love:
For it is in giving that we receive;
It is in pardoning that we are pardoned;
It is in dying that we awaken to eternal life.

ST FRANCIS OF ASSISI

17 April

Father, we praise you for giving us the institution of the family to illumine and reflect our relationship with the Creator and to share your love with others. By way of our divinely ordained roles as parents and children, we begin to fathom our position as sons and daughters of God, and brothers and sisters in Christ. And, as the Psalmist wrote, 'We will tell the next generation the praiseworthy deeds of the Lord … which He commanded our forefathers to teach their children, so the next generation would know them, even the children yet to be born, and they in turn would tell their children.' Thank you, Lord, for creating the family as the means by which the Good News is preached throughout the world.

JAMES DOBSON

18 April

O God, our strength, no flesh shall be justified in Thy sight. Who then shall stand before Thee? O Lord Jesus, our only refuge, our Saviour and our Deliverer, our hope is in Thee. Thou art our saving health. Thy lips have called us, and we have heard Thy voice. Thou hast guided us with Thy counsel; wilt Thou not also bring us to Thy glory? We beseech Thee, Almighty Father, we beseech Thee, O well-beloved Son of God, our merciful Redeemer, we beseech Thee, O Holy Spirit the Comforter, so lead and guide us, that at the last we may be brought unto Thy holy hill, and to Thy dwelling. Amen.

ANSELM

19 April

Almighty and ever-living God, the Father of our Lord Jesus Christ, who of Thine infinite goodness hast revealed Thyself unto us Thy creatures, and hast declared Thy goodwill towards us, and Thine unspeakable design for the redemption of mankind by the gift of Thine only begotten Son; have mercy upon us, and upon Thy whole Church; forgive us all the sins that we have committed against Thee, whether by negligence or ignorance, by omission or commission, or by reason of the weakness of human nature.

Pardon us, we beseech Thee, for the sake of Jesus Christ Thy Son, whom Thou hast appointed to be a sacrifice for us, a Mediator and Advocate.

PHILIP MELANCTHON

20 April

O Lord, my God, I adore and worship Thee. I ought to say, 'Depart from me for I am a sinful man.' But I cannot say that for I need Thee so desperately and there is nowhere else to go; no one else to whom to turn who really understands.

So I bow in Thy presence and in imagination I hear the seraphim – in voices awed and rapt and hushed by a solemnity that seems almost tangible, as though the place were filled with smoke – as they cry:

'HOLY, HOLY, HOLY,

is the Lord of Hosts. The whole earth is full of His glory.'

In this place made holy by Thy presence, with some fire from Thine altar, cleanse me. Grant that *my* iniquity may be taken away and *my* sin purged.

I thank Thee, O my God, for being what Thou eternally art.

LESLIE WEATHERHEAD

21 April

Glory be to Thee, O Lord, glory to Thee.
Creator of the light,
and Enlightener of the world –
of the visible light,
the Sun's ray, a flame of fire,
day and night,
evening and morning –
of the light invisible,
the revelation of God,
writings of the Law,
oracles of Prophets,
music of Psalms,
instruction of Proverbs,
experience of Histories –
light which never sets.
God is the Lord who hath shewed us light.
O by Thy resurrection raise us up
unto newness of life.
Up with our hearts;
we lift them to the Lord.

LANCELOT ANDREWES

22 April

O God, my God, I am all weakness, but Thou art my Strength; I am ever anew bowed down by any trial, but Thou canst and willest to lift me up. Let me not fail, O God, my Strength; let me not be discouraged, O God, my Hope. Draw me each day, if it be but a little nearer unto Thee; make me, each day, if it be but a little less unlike Thee; let me do or bear each day something, for love of Thee, whereby I may be fitter for Thee. Let no day pass without my having done something pleasing unto Thee. Thus alone would I live, that I may live more unto Thee; thus would I die, longing to love Thee more. Amen.

E. B. PUSEY

23 April

Almighty God, by whom alone kings reign and princes decree justice, and from whom alone cometh all counsel, wisdom, and understanding,

We, Thine unworthy servants, here gathered together in Thy name, do most humbly beseech Thee to send down the heavenly wisdom from above, to direct and guide us in all our consultations:

And grant that, we having Thy fear always before our eyes, and laying aside all private interests, prejudices, and partial affections, the result of all our counsels may be the glory of Thy blessed name, the maintenance of true religion and justice, and the safety, honour, and happiness of the King, the public welfare, peace and tranquillity of the realm, and the uniting and knitting together of the hearts of all persons and estates within the same in true Christian love and charity towards one another, Through Jesus Christ our Lord and Saviour.

HOUSE OF COMMONS PRAYER
(*composed by Sir Christopher Yelverton;*
Speaker of the House and MP for Northampton c. *1578*)

24 April

Make our hearts so right with Thy most holy and loving heart, that hoping in Thee we may do good; until that day when faith and hope shall be abolished by sight and possession, and love shall be all in all. Amen.

CHRISTINA ROSSETTI

25 April

Ah, Lord, unto Whom all hearts are open, Thou canst govern the vessel of my soul far better than I can. Arise, O Lord, and command the stormy wind and the troubled sea of my heart to be still, and at peace in Thee, that I may look up to Thee undisturbed, and abide in union with Thee, my Lord. Let me not be carried hither and thither by wandering thoughts; but, forgetting all else, let me see and hear Thee. Renew my spirit; kindle in me Thy light, that it may shine within me, and my heart may burn in love and adoration towards Thee. Let Thy Holy Spirit dwell in me continually, and make me Thy temple and sanctuary, and fill me with divine love and light and life, with devout and heavenly thoughts, with comfort and strength, with joy and peace. Amen.

JOHANN ARNDT

26 April

Great and Eternal God, before whom the angels veil their faces with their wings, and cry Holy, Holy, Holy, Lord God of Hosts – hear the poor and inarticulate murmurings of the most unworthy child in Thy great family. Cast me not away from Thy presence, and abandon me not to the evil that riots in my soul. Absolve me from my offences, and startle me into literal obedience of Thy holy commandments. I have done evil in Thy sight and have not thought upon Thy testimonies; spare me, O Lord, for Thy Son, my Saviour's sake. Cast down the barrier of sin that I have erected between myself and my God, and teach me Thy will; give me also the power and the will to order my life as will best please Thee, and glorify Thy name.

WALTER JAMES

27 April

My God, my God, why have you forsaken me?
Our God, our God, why have you forsaken us?
My God, our God, my Father, our Father
When will we ever learn, when will they ever learn?
God, my Father
I am filled
With anguish and puzzlement.
Why, O God, is there so much
Suffering, such needless suffering?
Everywhere we look there is pain
And suffering.

I don't understand, O God, my God,
Our God, O my Father, our Father,
Why, oh why, must there be so much
Pain and suffering in your creation so very good and
    beautiful?

DESMOND TUTU

28 April

Although we have sinned, yet have we an Advocate with the Father, Jesus Christ the righteous; and He is the propitiation for our sins. For He was wounded for our offences and smitten for our wickedness. Let us, therefore, return unto Him, who is the merciful receiver of all true penitent sinners.

BOOK OF COMMON PRAYER

Lord, enlighten us to see the beam that is in our own eye, and blind us to the mote that is in our brother's. Blind us to the offences of our beloved, cleanse them from our memories, take them out of our mouths for ever.

ROBERT LOUIS STEVENSON

29 April

Heavenly Father, I'm so glad that I can sincerely say that it's good to praise You and make music to Your Name, and to proclaim Your love in the morning and Your faithfulness at night. You have made me glad by Your love in the Lord Jesus, and all You have done for me in Him – and what You continue to do day by day. I want to sing for joy at Your goodness.

Help me in my singing to tell of all Your wonderful acts, and to contribute helpfully to the corporate praise of Your people. May I learn how to minister to others in the way in which I sing. To this end, may Your Spirit enable me to sing wholeheartedly, intelligently, and with my focus on Yourself and Your Son, the Lord Jesus.

DEREK PRIME

30 April

O Lord, strengthen our faith in Him who hath suffered on the cross for us. Teach us to walk according to His example. May we, like Him, be kind and compassionate, forbearing and forgiving, holy and harmless, undefiled and separate from sinners.

And bless us not this day only, but to the end of our lives. We pray, that so long as we remain in this world of trial, Thou wouldst strengthen us by Thy Holy Spirit, and comfort us, and continually direct us. Suffer us not, at any time, to depart from Thee, who art our Father, and our God, through any allurements of the world, or any temptations of the flesh, or of the Devil; but make us ever steadfast in Thy truth, and faithful to Thy cause, and devoted to Thy service.

We offer up these our imperfect prayers, in the name, and through the mediation, of our only Saviour, Jesus Christ.

HENRY THORNTON

1 May

O God, what a fool I am to live with a grudge when I can live with grace. If there are any grudges in my heart then I ask you to uproot them now. Cleanse me from every sin, I ask of you in Jesus' name.

I don't want to stumble around in the darkness, making myself and those I live with miserable. Help me to remove every trace of bitterness and hatred from my heart this day and walk in the light – the light of love.

Search my heart to see if there is any wicked way in me. I want to rise, from this moment, to a life of wholeness and obedience. Help me, dear Lord.

Heavenly Father, help me make generosity the basis of all my dealings with everyone I meet today. And not just today but every day. Help me be the channel, not the stopping place, of Your generosity. In Christ's name I ask it. Amen.

SELWYN HUGHES

2 May

Grant, we beseech Thee, merciful Father, that we may never presume on our own might and power; but, acknowledging our own infirmity, frailty, and weakness, may receive at Thy mighty hand strength to perform Thy holy and blessed will. Hear us, O Lord Jesus, for Thy name's sake.

THOMAS CRANMER

3 May

Lord, you are our Teacher,
and we would ask you to be kind to us,
your little children.
You are the Father, the Guide of Israel;
you are not only Son but Father too.
As we seek to be obedient,
may we become more like you,
and as far as it is possible,
may you be to us a good God and a merciful Judge.

May we all live in your peace;
and as we journey towards your dwelling-place,
carried calmly along by the Holy Spirit.
Day and night until the final day,
may we thank you and praise you constantly:
you who are both Father and Son,
Son and Father,
the Son who is our Teacher and our Guide,
together with the Holy Spirit.

CLEMENT OF ALEXANDRIA

4 May

O Almighty and Everlasting God, how terrible is this world, it openeth its mouth to swallow me up, and I have so little trust in Thee. How weak is the flesh – and Satan how strong! Faithful and Unchangeable God, help me against all the wisdom of the world. In no man do I vainly put my trust, all of man is uncertain, all that cometh of man fails. Hearest Thou me not? Art Thou dead? No, Thou only hidest Thyself. Thou hast chosen me for this work. Act then O God! Stand at my side, for the sake of Thy Well-Beloved Jesus Christ, Who is my Defence, my Shield and my Strong Tower.

MARTIN LUTHER

5 May

God, thou art greatly in favour of Revival. Thou art now stirring up the sainthood to pray for what you favour. Our every other need sinks into insignificance compared to the need of a deep and widespread old-time Revival.

A Revival that will fill the hearts of saints with holy love and so burden the hearts of God's ministers that the Word of God will be like fire shut up in their bones.

A Revival that will make both the Church and the world realise the shortness of time and the importance of eternity.

A Revival that has so much of heaven and so much of God's glory in it that all the world will be compelled to see and feel its mighty influence.

A PRAYER FOR REVIVAL (PART ONE)
(*An excerpt from a prayer published in 1904
in* Old Time Religion *Magazine*)

6 May

Whom have we, O God, in heaven but Thee? And there is none upon earth that we desire besides Thee. Our flesh and our heart faileth; but Thou art the strength of our heart, and our portion for ever.

We worship Thee as the greatest and best of Beings, the perfection of all excellence, and the source of all goodness. And we beseech Thee to manifest Thyself to us, in the adorable attributes of Thy character, and in the exceeding abundance of Thy tender mercies, so that we may be led more heartily to love Thee, and more worthily to magnify Thy blessed name.

PRAYERS FOR SOCIAL AND FAMILY WORSHIP
(*by the Church of Scotland*)

7 May

Lord, teach me the art of patience whilst I am well, and give me the use of it when I am sick. In that day either lighten my burden or strengthen my back. Make me, who so often in my health have discovered my weakness presuming on my own strength, to be strong in my sickness when I solely rely on Thy assistance.

THOMAS FULLER

Lord, where we are wrong
make us willing to change,
And where we are right
make us easy to live with.

PETER MARSHALL

8 May

Father, your word says that Christ came into the world to save sinners. I am a sinner and I believe that Jesus died on the cross for me. You have said that whoever comes to you will not be cast out; so I come claiming the finished work of Christ, humbly asking that you will be to me all that I need. The Bible contains the promise that you will never leave me nor forsake me, so I journey through the complexities of this life in the peace of your presence, peace that the world cannot give or take away. Father, I have read that in you is fullness of joy; bring me deeper into you I pray in Jesus' name. Amen.

ROBERT AMESS

9 May

Oh! bring us, we pray Thee, now near to Thyself. Let us bathe ourselves in communion with our God. Blessed be the love which chose us before the world began. We can never sufficiently adore Thee for Thy sovereignty, the sovereignty of love which saw us in the ruins of the Fall, yet loved us notwithstanding all.

We praise the God of the Eternal Council Chamber and of the Everlasting Covenant, but where shall we find sufficiently fit words with which to praise Him who gave us grace in Christ His Son, before He spread the starry sky?

We also bless Thee, O God, as the God of our redemption, for Thou hast so loved us as to give even Thy dear Son for us. He gave Himself, His very life for us that He might redeem us from all iniquity and separate us unto Himself to be His peculiar people, zealous for good works.

C. H. SPURGEON

10 May

Father in Heaven, Thou hast not left the world, or us all, or any one of us alone. When we were fallen away from Thee and were lost, Thou didst seek and find us by making reconciliation through Thy dear Son Jesus Christ, by opening a way for us, and by giving us hope. Do not look now at our sin, but at Thy grace. Give us Thy Spirit, that we may be well pleasing to Thee. Grant that we may pray to Thee with all our heart, and joyously praise Thee with our lips.

All this we pray through Jesus Christ, our Lord. Amen.

KARL BARTH

11 May

O Lord Jesus Christ, who has created and redeemed me, and has brought me to that which now I am; you know what you would do with me; do with me according to your will, for your tender mercy's sake. Amen.

HENRY VI

Almighty God, Whom the eye cannot behold, and Whom we cannot hear with the hearing of the ear, still let us this day feel Thy Presence and know Thy Love, and being stirred and moved above ourselves, thus be lifted into the knowledge of God and the bearing of His holy way.

GEORGE DAWSON

12 May

O Eternal God, the great Father of spirits, the great Lover of souls, who didst send Thy Holy Spirit upon Thy Church in the day of Pentecost, and hast promised that He shall abide with the Church for ever; let Thy Holy Spirit lead us into all truth, defend us from all sin, enrich us with His gifts, refresh us with His comforts, rule in our hearts for ever, conduct us with His truth, and lead us in the way everlasting; that we, living by Thy Spirit and walking in Him, may by Him be sealed unto the day of our redemption. Let Thy Spirit witness to our spirits that we are the children of God; and keep us so for ever, through Jesus Christ our Lord, who liveth and reigneth with Thee in the unity of the same Spirit, one God, world without end. Amen.

JEREMY TAYLOR

13 May

Let Thy will be mine, and my will ever follow Thine in perfect agreement with it, so that I may neither choose nor reject, save what Thou choosest and rejectest.

Grant me to die to all that is in the world, and for love of Thee to be content to be despised and unknown in this life.

HENRY S. LUNN

O Lord, how I long for a great flood of Thy generous-heartedness in and through all things; pour in, O Lord, Thy water of life. May the power and sweetness and tone and health of God go through me this day.

OSWALD CHAMBERS

14 May

Receive us evermore into Thy protection, maintaining and increasing from day to day Thy grace and goodness towards us, until Thou hast brought us unto the full and perfect unity of Thy son, Jesus Christ, our Lord, who is the true light of our souls.

And to the end that we may obtain these requests at Thy hands, may it please Thee also to forget all our sins past, and of Thy infinite mercy freely to pardon them, according as Thou hast promised to all them that call upon Thee with a true heart. Grant us these our petitions, O Father of mercy; for our Lord and Saviour, Jesus Christ's sake. Amen.

LITURGY OF GENEVA

15 May

This, O Father, is life everlasting, to know Thee, the only True God, and Jesus Christ whom Thou hast sent. And therefore, we pray Thee, increase our faith, that this knowledge may evermore dwell in us: increase our obedience, that we may not swerve from Thy commandments, and increase our firm hold of Thee, that we may forget the things which are behind, and reach forward to those which are before, and go on unto perfection. Multiply Thy grace upon us, that being daily more dead unto sin and alive unto Thee, we may be constantly led by Thy Holy Spirit: fearing Thee only, who art most worthy to be feared; glorying in Thee only, who art the glory of all Thy saints; desiring nothing but Thee, who art of all things the worthiest and the best; and, at last, living and dwelling with Thee.

DESIDERIUS ERASMUS

16 May

Heavenly Father, I thank You for watching over me during the night. Keep me this day from all that is hurtful to soul and body. Teach me to fear and love You above all things. Make me dutiful and loving to those I meet and to all who are placed over me. When tempted to be angry, may I remember that a soft answer turns away wrath. Help me by Your Holy Spirit to shun bad company, to speak the truth at all times, and to be honest in will and deed. Bless all whom I love and help me so to live in this world that I may have everlasting life, through Jesus Christ our Lord.

MAURICE ROWLANDSON

17 May

Great art Thou, O Lord, and greatly to be praised; great is Thy power, and Thy wisdom is infinite. Thee would we praise without ceasing. Thou callest us to delight in Thy praise; for Thou hast made us for Thyself, and our hearts find no rest until we rest in Thee.

Almighty Father, enter Thou our hearts, and so fill us with Thy love, that forsaking all evil desires, we may embrace Thee our only good. Show unto us, for Thy mercies' sake, O Lord our God, what Thou art unto us. Say unto our souls, I am thy salvation. So speak that we may hear. Our hearts are before Thee; open Thou our ears; let us hasten after Thy voice, and take hold on Thee. Hide not Thy face from us, we beseech Thee, O Lord.

ST AUGUSTINE

18 May

O Merciful God, be Thou now unto me a strong tower of
defence, I humbly entreat Thee. Give me grace to await
Thy leisure, and patiently to bear what Thou doest unto
me; nothing doubting or mistrusting Thy goodness
towards me; for Thou knowest what is good for me better
than I do. Therefore do with me in all things what Thou
wilt; only arm me, I beseech Thee, with thine armour, that
I may stand fast; above all things, taking to me the shield of
faith; praying always that I may refer myself wholly to Thy
will, abiding Thy pleasure, and comforting myself in those
troubles which it shall please Thee to send me, seeing such
troubles are profitable for me; and I am assuredly persuaded
that all Thou doest cannot but be well, and unto Thee be all
honour and glory. Amen.

LADY JANE GREY

19 May

Blessed be Thou, Lord God our Father, for ever and ever. Thine, O Lord, is the greatness and the power, and the glory, and the victory, and the majesty: for all that is in the heaven and in the earth is Thine: Thine is the Kingdom, O Lord, and Thou art exalted as Head above all. Both riches and honour come of Thee, and Thou reignest over all: and In Thine hand is power and might: and in Thine hand it is to make great, and to give strength unto all. Now, therefore, our God, we thank Thee, and praise Thy glorious Name. Amen.

BOOK OF CONGREGATIONAL PRAYER, 1920

20 May

O Lord who alone can do for us
  the good things we ask and more also,
to you we give thanks
  through the High Priest and Champion of our souls,
Jesus Christ,
through whom to you
  be glory and majesty
both now and for generations of generations
  and to the ages of ages.
Amen.

ST CLEMENT OF ROME

Deal Thou with me, O Lord, according to Thy Name, for sweet is Thy mercy.

In the multitude of the sorrows I had in my heart, Thy comforts have refreshed my soul.

Unto Thy entire disposal I resign my spirit, for Thou hast redeemed me, O Lord, thou God of truth.

THOMAS KEN

21 May

Lord Jesus, I feel lonely. Most of what I valued is gone. Loss seems to surround me like a great wide ocean, leaving me cut off on an island, quite alone. Loss on all sides, loss in every direction. All I can hear are the echoes of familiar voices and laughter from the past. The memories of all the things I wanted to do, places I wanted to visit, people I wanted to meet, merely mock me now that I am stranded here in this desolate place.

You must have been lonely so often, because the people you loved best always seemed to misunderstand what you said and did.

So, because you understand, will you come into my loneliness and share it with me? Then, because I know I am not alone after all, please give me the courage to stop excluding other people. They could be the very ones you might be sending to me, friends who are willing to be your arms to comfort me. Lord, please help me.

JENNIFER REES LARCOMBE

22 May

Almighty God, unto Whom all hearts be open, all desires known, and from Whom no secrets are hid; cleanse the thoughts of our hearts by the inspiration of Thy Holy Spirit, that we may perfectly love Thee and worthily magnify Thy holy name. Through Christ our Lord. Amen.

BOOK OF COMMON PRAYER

O Christ of pure and perfect love,
Look on this sin-stained heart of mine!
I thirst Thy cleansing grace to prove,
I want my life to be like Thine.
O see me at Thy footstool bow.
And come and sanctify me now!

WILLIAM BOOTH

23 May

Praise the Lord, you children
praise the Name of the Lord.
We praise you,
we sing to you,
we bless you,
for your great glory,
O Lord our King,
Father of Christ – the spotless Lamb,
who takes away the sin of the world.

Praise becomes you,
worship becomes you,
glory becomes you,
God and Father,
through your Son,
in the Holy Spirit,
for ever and ever.
Amen.

APOSTOLIC

24 May

Almighty God, our heavenly Father, the privilege is
ours to share in the loving, healing, reconciling mission
of your Son Jesus Christ, our Lord, in this age and where-
ever we are. Since without you we can do no good thing.
    May your Spirit make us wise;
    May your Spirit guide us;
    May your Spirit renew us;
    May your Spirit strengthen us;
So that we will be:
    Strong in faith,
    Discerning in proclamation,
    Courageous in witness,
    Persistent in good deeds.
This we ask through the name of the Father.

A PRAYER FROM THE CHURCH OF THE
PROVINCE OF THE WEST INDIES

25 May

Great and marvellous are Thy works, O Lord God Almighty; just and true are Thy ways, Thou King of saints ...

Blessed Jesus, grant us Thy grace ... Teach us to desire always that which is acceptable to Thee, and to enjoy in Thee that peace which the world cannot give.

The path of this life has been sanctified by Thy footsteps, and through Thee the weak are made strong. The narrow way, though painful, has been made plain and easy, since Thou didst condescend to tread it on our behalf ... Enable us by Thy grace to do that which without Thee is impossible. Teach us to glory in tribulations also, knowing that to suffer according to Thy will worketh patience, and patience experience, and experience hope, even that which maketh not ashamed. Amen.

THOMAS À KEMPIS

26 May

Holy Father, we give thanks unto Thee for all Thou art to us, and for all Thou doest for us day by day. For reason and conscience, for nurture and guidance, and for all the gifts of nature and of grace; for Thy forbearance and long-suffering, and Thy tender mercies which never fail: for every benefit bestowed, for Thy promise and our hope of good for time to come: for these and all other mercies, known and unknown, remembered or forgotten, we will give thanks unto Thee now and evermore. Amen.

BOOK OF CONGREGATIONAL PRAYER, 1920

27 May

Gracious Father, we thank you that in every circumstance of life we can trust in your providential care for your children; guiding, overruling and protecting. You work all things together for our good, as you know it to be. Help us to trust you when the circumstances of our lives are difficult, to turn to you when we are tempted to turn away, and to deepen our relationship with you as a result. And through all the challenges of life help us to become more like Jesus because we ask it in his Name. Amen.

WALLACE BENN

28 May

Blessed Lord, Thy words are faithful and true. It must be because I pray amiss that my experience of answered prayer is not clearer. It must be because I live too little in the Spirit that my prayer is too little in the Spirit, and that the power for the prayer of faith is wanting. Lord, teach me to pray! Lord Jesus, I trust Thee for it; teach me to pray in faith.

ANDREW MURRAY

O Lord, do Thou create in our hearts a sincere desire to become better, and a steadfast resolution to endeavour to grow in grace and in the knowledge of Jesus Christ our Lord. Amen.

SYMON PATRICK

29 May

O Lord God Almighty, we pray Thee now to deliver us from all wandering thoughts. Help us to remember in whose presence we are; and enable us to worship Thee in spirit and in truth.

O Lord, our Heavenly Father, who art the preserver of our lives and the giver of all the good things which we enjoy, we thank Thee for the mercies of the past night. We bless Thy Name that we are here in so much health and comfort: and that we have now the prospect of passing another day in the enjoyment of the bounties of Thy providence; while we have also set before us the blessed hope of everlasting life. We beseech Thee to give us this day grace to serve Thee and to walk according to the Gospel of Jesus Christ.

HENRY THORNTON

30 May

O God the Father Almighty, Creator and Governor of all things; O God the Son Eternal, our Redeemer, Intercessor and Judge; O God the Holy Ghost, the Sanctifier, Who with the Father and the Son together art worshipped and glorified, have mercy upon us. Pardon, O Lord, the sins and offences of our past lives, for Thy mercy's sake; from pride and vanity, from selfishness and envy, from love of the world and forgetfulness of Thee, good Lord, deliver us. We beseech Thee to hear us, O Lord, for all who are in trouble, suffering, or distress; for the needy and them that have no helper; for the sick, the dying, and the mourners. For our relations, friends and benefactors; for our enemies, persecutors and slanderers; for all with whom we live or have to do. Hear us, O Lord, we humbly beseech Thee, for the sake of Jesus Christ the Son of God. Amen.

ANCIENT LITANY

31 May

Come, true light.
Come, life eternal.
Come, hidden mystery.
Come, treasure without name.
Come, reality beyond all words.
Come, person beyond all understanding.
Come, rejoicing without end.
Come, light that knows no evening.
Come, unfailing expectation of the saved.
Come, raising of the fallen.
Come, resurrection of the dead.
Come, all powerful, for unceasingly you create, refashion and change all things by your will alone.
Come, invisible whom none may touch and handle.
Come, for your name fills our hearts with longing and is ever on our lips; yet who you are and what your nature is, we cannot say or know.
Come, Alone to the alone.
Come, for you are yourself the desire that is within me.
Come, my breath and my life.
Come, the consolation of my humble soul.
Come, my joy, my glory, my endless delight.

ST SYMEON THE NEW THEOLOGIAN

1 June

Come quickly to help me, O Lord God of my salvation, for the battle is great and the adversaries are powerful. The enemy is hostile, the invisible foe fighting through visible forms. Come quickly, therefore, to help us, and assist us through your Holy Son, our Lord Jesus Christ, through whom you have redeemed us all, through whom be glory and power to you for ever and ever. Amen.

ORIGEN

O God, without thee we are not able to please thee; mercifully grant that thy Holy Spirit may in all things direct and rule our hearts; through Jesus Christ our Lord. Amen.

BOOK OF COMMON PRAYER

2 June

Today I bought a walking stick. O Jesus, it wasn't the happiest of purchases; dancing shoes would have pleased me better, but people with MS don't wear dancing shoes. Weak and weary, I need the stick to steady the same feet that used to whirl about to music, such an exhilarating way to praise You, laughing and gasping to catch up with my own breath.

Lord, I still want to worship You. As I stumble from the house with this crutch, You are there beside me and perhaps I'll see and hear You more distinctly than in the glorious flurry of dance. There is always grace in every circumstance. Please help me not to miss it. Amen.

CELIA BOWRING

3 June

Dear Lord, please infuse me with your joy. Put a radiant smile on my face and let me see the privilege of further training. Help me to truly praise You in these circumstances; may tears of thankfulness and release flow freely. Give us Your continued grace and courage, and remove the fear that comes in the night watches. Deepen our love, O Lord, and grant us such an anointing that others will be deeply impacted even though they are not aware of it happening. Amen.

LYNDON BOWRING

4 June

Father in heaven, I thank you that you have set me apart for Your own personal use. You have called me to be a witness to Jesus, to be a fisher of men, to be a disciple maker, to be a church builder.

Help me not to be ashamed of the gospel of Christ, for it is the power of salvation, and strengthen me to take every opportunity to declare it. Give me a deep and abiding longing for all hurting people to experience Christ's saving love.

Give me an ever increasing experience of your holy anointing. Grant that I may always depend on your power and not my own ability for I am but an earthen vessel.

In the blessed name of Jesus. Amen.

COLIN DYE

5 June

Lord, in your mercy and grace,
reach out your hand and heal those that are sick.
Restore their health,
deliver them from the sicknesses they now have.

Heal them in the Name of your only Son;
let his holy Name be their cure,
may it restore them to health and wholeness;
by him may power and glory be yours, in the Holy Spirit,
as they shall be,
age after age.
Amen.

SERAPION OF THMUIS EUCHOLOGIUM

Of all the gifts thine hand bestows,
  Thou giver of all good!
Not heaven itself a richer knows,
  Than my Redeemer's blood.

WILLIAM COWPER

6 June

O Lord Jesus Christ, Who didst agonise in Gethsemane, and drink for us the awful cup of suffering; inflame our hearts with ever increasing love to Thee. Help us to know the fellowship of Thy sufferings, and grant that we, following the example of Thy patience, may be ready also to forgive to the uttermost all who sin against us, for Thy name's sake. Amen.

THOMAS HALL

From the cowardice that dare not face new truths,
From the laziness that is contented with half truths,
From the arrogance that thinks it knows all truth,
Good Lord deliver me.

BREAD FOR TOMORROW
(*a prayer from Kenya*)

7 June

O most merciful Father, since we know not what we should pray for as we ought, grant us the help of Thy Holy Spirit; that He may teach us to pray.

We lift up our eyes unto Thee, O Thou that dwellest in the heavens. O Spirit of God, so teach and quicken us that we may pray unto Thee, not with the lips only, but with our whole heart and our whole soul. May we call upon Thee, not in hypocrisy, but worshipping Thee in spirit and in truth. So teach us, that we may ask of Thee such things as are agreeable to Thy holy will.

Grant our petitions for His sake, who is at Thy right hand, ever making intercession for us. To Him, with Thyself, and the Holy Ghost, be equal and undivided praise. Amen.

DESIDERIUS ERASMUS

8 June

O Lord, let Thy peace rule in our hearts, and may it be our strength and our song. We commit ourselves to Thy care and keeping this day; let Thy grace be mighty in us, and let it work in us both to will and to do of Thine own good pleasure, and grant us strength for all the duties of the day. Keep us from sin. Give us the rule over our own spirits, and keep us from speaking unadvisedly with our lips. May we live together in peace and holy love, and do Thou command Thy blessing upon us.

Prepare us for all the events of the day, for we know not what a day may bring forth. Give us grace to deny ourselves; to take up our cross daily, and to follow in the steps of our Lord and Master, Jesus Christ our Lord. Amen.

MATTHEW HENRY

9 June

Holy Spirit, make my heart Thy home, and dwell with me for evermore. Teach me what Thou art; show Thyself to me, my Friend and Comforter. Give me a deeper interest in Thy dealings with men; and if I only know a little of Thy wondrous secrets let that little be the truth, and nothing but the truth. Help me so to live that my soul and body may be a fit temple for Thy glory, and a useful instrument for Thy power.

WALTER JAMES

10 June

Lord, I come to kneel at Your feet and worship You. You are the Almighty, the Maker of mighty galaxies and tiny atoms, and You keep track of them all. This leaves me awestruck and slightly nervous. And yet, as I kneel here, I dare to look up and call You Father because You have made me Your child through what You did at the Cross. I love You for it, dear Lord, and it makes me so safe to know that You love me with the same love with which You love Your Son Jesus.

Because I love You, I want to spend my life serving You and fulfilling Your heart's desires. Let us work together in saving souls and building Your Church. Grant that Your Holy Spirit will help me to do so; then, You will be pleased, and so will I.

I look forward to serving You all my days, and then I shall be with You forever in your Home. Oh God, how glorious that will be: it excites me, it motivates me, and makes me a bit impatient to get there.

ALEX BUCHANAN

11 June

O Lord my God,
my one hope,
   hear me,
that weariness may not lessen my will to seek you,
that I may seek your face ever more with eager heart.

Lord, give me strength to seek you,
as you have made me to find you,
and given me hope of finding you ever more and more.

My strength and my weakness are in your hands:
preserve the one, and remedy the other.
In your hands
   are my knowledge and my ignorance.
Where you have opened to me,
   receive my entering in.
Where you have shut,
   open to my knocking.

Let me remember you,
   understand you,
   love you.
Increase in me all these,
   until you restore me to your perfect pattern.

ST AUGUSTINE

12 June

Into Thine hands I commend
my spirit, soul and body,
which Thou hast created, redeemed, regenerated,
O Lord, Thou God of truth;
and together with me
all mine and all that belongs to me.
Lord, in Thy goodness,
guard us from all evil,
guard our souls,
I beseech Thee, O Lord.
Guard us without falling,
and place us immaculate
in the presence of Thy glory
in that day.
Guard my going out and my coming in
henceforth and for ever.
Prosper, I pray Thee, Thy servant this day,
and grant him mercy
in the sight of those who meet him.
O God, make speed to save me,
O Lord, make haste to help me.

LANCELOT ANDREWES

13 June

Ever-changing edicts not only of scientists but also of philosophers and even theologians can be disappointingly transient. But from everlasting to everlasting you are the eternal God through whom we are offered the surety of everlasting life already in this world as well as in the world to come. By faith in Christ, your crucified, risen and returning Son, we are offered forgiveness of sins and eternal life, and enablement by the Holy Spirit for lives well-pleasing to you and your purposes.

CARL T. H. HENRY

14 June

Pardon, O Lord, our offences, voluntarily or involuntarily, wittingly or unwittingly committed, by word or deed, or in thought: Forgive those that are hidden, and those that are manifest; those that were done long ago, those which are known, and those which are forgotten but are known unto Thee. Forgive, O God, through Jesus Christ our Lord. Amen.

LITURGY OF SYRIAN JACOBITES

Lord, keep me ever near to Thee. Let nothing separate me from Thee, let nothing keep me back from Thee. If I fall, bring me back quickly to Thee, and make me hope in Thee, trust in Thee, love Thee everlastingly. Amen.

E. B. PUSEY

15 June

Holy Father, thank You for helping me to understand that I can praise You as much in the ordinary affairs of life as in the unusual and more exciting things.

Thank You that through the Lord Jesus – and through Him alone – I can continually offer to You a sacrifice of praise. I want to praise You as much by my attitudes as by my words and my actions.

In the light of Your mercy to me, I want to do everything for the Lord Jesus.

I commit myself now – with Your Spirit's help – to greater thankfulness, more wholehearted work, greater diligence in pursuing holiness and Christlikeness, and joy in giving; please bring greater praise to Your Name from my life by these and any other means You choose. For Jesus' sake. Amen.

DEREK PRIME

16 June

Our Father, Thy children who know Thee delight themselves in Thy presence. We are never happier than when we are near Thee. We have found a little heaven in prayer.

We thank Thee, Lord, that we have not only found benefit in prayer, but in the answers to it. Thou hast supplied our necessities as soon as ever we have cried unto Thee; yea, we have found it true: 'Before they call I will answer, and while they are yet speaking I will hear.'

We do bless Thee, Lord, for instituting the blessed ordinance of prayer. What could we do without it, and we take great shame to ourselves that we should use it so little. We pray that we may be men of prayer, taken up with it, that it may take us up and bear us as on its wings towards heaven.

Let the benediction of heaven descend on men, through Jesus Christ our Lord. Amen.

C. H. SPURGEON

17 June

O Holy Spirit,
Grant me the faith that will protect me from despair:
Deliver me from the lust of the flesh.
Pour into my heart such love for Thee and for all men that
hatred and bitterness may be blotted out.
Grant me the hope that will deliver me from fear and
timidity.
O Holy and Merciful God,
Creator and Redeemer,
Judge and Saviour,
Thou knowest me and all that I do.
Thou hatest and dost punish evil without respect of persons
in this world and the next.
Thou forgivest the sins of them that heartily pray for
forgiveness.
Thou lovest goodness and rewardest it on this earth with a
clear conscience,
and in the world to come with a crown of righteousness.

DIETRICH BONHOEFFER

18 June

Dear Jesus, help me to spread Your fragrance
    everywhere I go.
Flood my soul with Your spirit and life.
Penetrate and possess my whole being, so utterly,
    that my life may only be a radiance of Yours.
Shine through me, and be so in me,
    that every soul I come in contact with
    may feel Your presence in my soul.
Let them look up and see no longer me,
    but only Jesus!
Stay with me, and then I shall begin to shine as You shine;
So to shine as to be a light to others.

JOHN HENRY NEWMAN

19 June

Come, my Light, and illumine my darkness.
Come, my Life, and revive me from death.
Come, my Physician, and heal my wounds.
Come, Flame of divine love, and burn up the
    thorns of my sins, kindling my heart with the
    flame of thy love.
Come, my King, sit upon the throne of my heart
    and reign there.
For thou alone art my King and my Lord.

ST DIMITRI OF RASTOV

Into Thy hands we commend ourselves, for Thou hast
redeemed us. Thou, Lord, Who hast redeemed us all for
Thine own sake, sanctify and save us this day. Amen.

CHRISTINA ROSSETTI

20 June

O Lord Jesus Christ, who art the Way, the Truth, and the Life, we pray Thee suffer us not to stray from Thee, who art the Way, nor to distrust Thee, who art the Truth, nor to rest in any other things than Thee, who art the Life. Teach us, by Thy Holy Spirit, what to believe, what to do, and wherein to take up our rest.

DESIDERIUS ERASMUS

O God, forasmuch as our strength is in Thee, mercifully grant that Thy Holy Spirit may in all things direct and rule our hearts, through Jesus Christ our Lord. Amen.

GELASIAN SACRAMENTARY

21 June

Lord, it is on a day like this I sometimes wonder how much I have allowed your grace to make a major change in my life.

Lord, teach me to love your word, to obey your commands, to submit to your Spirit and to die to this cruel self.

Thank you that victory is not only possible but is essential or else my life is little different from the people I meet each day who do not know You. Lord, I know the theory and a great amount of theology; help me to see it happen in my experience.

Thank you for all the prayers you have answered in the past; they have been beyond my best expectations. You are a great God and I worship you. Amen.

GEORGE RUSSELL

22 June

Almighty God, our heavenly Father, Thou art pleased to be acknowledged the Saviour of all men by the redemption accomplished by Jesus Christ. Be Thou, O Lord, our guide and protector throughout this day. Strengthen and fortify us against all the assaults of the devil, and deliver us from all the dangers of this life. Show us the way wherein we should walk, for we lift up our souls unto Thee. Teach us to do Thy will, for Thou art our God: let Thy good Spirit lead us forth into the land of uprightness.

Grant these petitions, O merciful Father, for Thy dear Son's sake, Jesus Christ, our Lord. Amen.

JOHN CALVIN

23 June

Almighty and ever blessed God, we thank thee that thy love never faileth. We thank thee, O Lord, that whenever we come truly unto thee, acknowledging our sin and looking only unto Jesus Christ and his blood, thou dost ever pardon us and forgive us and renew us and restore us. Hear us, then, O Lord, and glorify thy name in our midst and unto thee shall we give all the praise and all the honour and all the glory. Hear us, O Lord, and pardon and forgive us all our every sin as we ask these mercies, pleading nothing but the name and the merit of thy Son, our Lord and Saviour Jesus Christ. Amen.

D. MARTYN LLOYD-JONES

24 June

O God, my Father, I see that when problems come I need not whine or complain. I can make music out of misery, a song out of sorrow and success out of every setback.

I feel sad when I think of the number of times I have failed to thank those through whom your blessings have come into my life – Your agents. From now on I must be more sensitive and alert. Help me, dear Father.

Father, forgive me if I go through the day overlooking the common blessings of life. Help me develop keen sight so that I do not miss one of the multiplicity of Your benefits to me. Give me a thankful heart, dear Lord.

What will You give me today that I might offer back to You in thanksgiving, in praise and adoration? Help me not to miss one single thing. In Jesus' Name. Amen.

SELWYN HUGHES

25 June

Almighty God, Holy Spirit, who proceeds from the Father and the Son, and by the Eternal Son, our Redeemer, was promised unto us, to kindle in us the true knowledge and love of God, stir up in our hearts, we beseech Thee, true fear, true faith, and acknowledgement of the mercy which the Father of our Lord Jesus Christ hath promised unto us for His sake. Be Thou our comforter in all difficulties and dangers, and so kindle Divine love in our hearts, that by true obedience we may offer perpetual praise to Thyself, and to the Father of our Lord Jesus Christ, and to His blessed Son, our Redeemer. Amen.

PHILIP MELANCTHON

26 June

O Lord, we beseech thee to deliver us from the fear of the unknown future; from fear of failure; from fear of poverty; from fear of bereavement; from fear of loneliness; from fear of sickness and pain; from fear of age; and from fear of death. Help us, O Father, by thy grace to love and fear thee only; fill our hearts with cheerful courage and loving trust in thee; through our Lord and Master Jesus Christ.

AKANU IBAIM

Dear Lord, I wonder and adore!
    Thy grace is all divine!
O keep me, that I sin no more
    Against such love as thine!

JOHN NEWTON

27 June

O Father, in these hours of daylight we remember those who must wake that we may sleep; bless those who watch over us at night, the guardians of the peace, the watchers who guard us from the terrors of fire, with all the many who carry on through the hours of the night the restless commerce of man on land and sea. We thank Thee for their faithfulness and sense of duty; we pray Thee for pardon if our covetousness or luxury makes their nightly toil necessary. Grant that we may realise how dependent the safety of our loved ones, and the comforts of life, are upon these our brothers, so that we may think of them with love and gratitude, and help to make their burdens lighter, for the sake of Jesus Christ our Lord. Amen.

WALTER RAUSCHENBUSCH

28 June

To thank you properly
   is impossible;
to thank you according to our ability
   is right and proper.
For you have redeemed us
   from the waste of worshipping many gods,
   delivering us from error and ignorance.
You sent Christ as a human being among humans,
Christ who is the Only-Begotten God.

You have caused the Holy Spirit to dwell in us.
You have given your angels charge over us;
   you have put the devil to shame.
When we were not, you made us.
You take care of us when we are made;
   you measure out life to us;
   you provide us with food;
   you have promised repentance.

For all these things
   glory and worship be to you
through Jesus Christ, now, and for ever,
   and throughout all ages.
Amen.

APOSTOLIC CONSTITUTIONS

29 June

O Lord God, I thank Thee that Thou leadest me by a way which I know not, by a way which is above the level of my poor understanding. I thank Thee that Thou art not repelled by my bitterness, that Thou are not turned aside by the heat of my spirit. There is no force in this universe so glorious as the force of Thy love; it compels me to come in. O divine servitude, O slavery that makes me free, O love that imprisons me only to set my feet in a larger room, enclose me more and more within Thy folds. Protect me from the impetuous desires of my nature – desires as short-lived as they are impetuous. Ask me not where I would like to go; tell me where to go; lead me in Thine own way; hold me in Thine own light. Amen.

GEORGE MATHESON

30 June

Help us to look back on the long way that Thou hast brought us, on the long days in which we have been served, our feet have been plucked out from the blackness of despair, the horror of misconduct. For our sins forgiven or prevented, for our shame unpublished, we bless and thank Thee, O God. Help us yet again and ever. So order events, so strengthen our frailty, as that day by day we shall come before Thee with this song of gratitude, and in the end we be dismissed with honour. In their weakness and their fear, the vessels of thy handiwork so pray to Thee, so praise Thee. Amen.

ROBERT LOUIS STEVENSON

July 1

Grant to us, O Lord, to know that which is worth knowing, to love that which is worth loving, to praise that which can bear with praise, to hate what in thy sight is unworthy, to prize what to thee is precious, and above all to search out and to do what is well-pleasing unto thee: through Jesus Christ our Lord. Amen.

THOMAS À KEMPIS

Father, You know how much I need to be filled with Your strength. You know how weak I am in myself. Thank You that it is possible to be strong in You.

CORRIE TEN BOOM

2 July

God of our life, there are days when the burdens we carry chafe our shoulders and weigh us down; when the road seems weary and endless; the skies grey and threatening; when our lives have no music in them; and our hearts are lonely; and our souls have lost their courage. Flood the path with light, we beseech Thee; turn our eyes to where the skies are full of promise; tune our hearts to brave music; give us the sense of comradeship with heroes and saints of every age, and so quicken our spirit that we may be able to encourage the souls of all who journey with us on the road to Thy house and glory. Amen.

ACTS OF DEVOTION

3 July

O Thou Most High, make us to abide under the shadow of the Almighty. Bless us with Thy presence, Thy grace, and Thy protection. Do not allow the enemy to have any advantage over us; neither let the son of wickedness approach to hurt us.

Be with all Thy people everywhere; may those who are near and dear to us be near and dear to Thee; and whatever separation Thy good providence may ordain for us on earth, may we meet with joy at Thy right hand, at the appearing of our Lord and Saviour, Jesus Christ.

We beseech Thee to hear us, and grant us these and all other mercies, spiritual and temporal, only for the sake of Jesus Christ the righteous. Amen.

AUGUSTUS TOPLADY

4 July

Father – as sincere as we know how to be we come before you, in perpetual awe of your sovereignty and goodness, your mercy and judgement, your love and grace. Bring humility to our hearts to break our pride. Use us for your glory. Let the cross remain always at the forefront of our thoughts and deeds. Let us be conformed to your cross, Lord Jesus, that through your death we may obtain life through your resurrection. Be with us this day and guide the thoughts and intents of our hearts. For we desire your Holy Spirit to constantly dwell with us to guide us. In Christ's Name, Amen.

PAUL CAIN

5 July

O Trinity, uncreated and without beginning,
O undivided Unity, three and one,
Father, Son and Spirit, a single God:
Accept this our hymn from tongues of clay
As if from mouths of flame.

LENTEN TRIODION

Almighty and everlasting God, the Comfort of the sad, the
Strength of sufferers, let the prayers of those that cry out of
any tribulation come unto Thee, that all may rejoice to find
that Thy mercy is present with them in their afflictions;
through Jesus Christ our Lord. Amen.

GELASIAN SACRAMENTARY

6 July

O Shepherd of the sheep, who didst promise to carry the lambs in Thine arms, and to lead us by the still waters, help us to know the peace which passeth understanding. Give us that heavenly drink which is life, the calm patience which is content to bear what God giveth. Have mercy upon us, and hear our prayers. Lead us gently when we pass through the valley of the shadow of death. Guide us, till at last, in the assembly of Thy saints, we may find rest for evermore. Amen.

GEORGE DAWSON

7 July

O My Father, Thou Infinite One! My strength is weakness and I am not able to plead the cause of Your love. O plead Your own cause and what heart can resist! Let it not be my work only, but Yours that You love me, even me, a sinner! Tell me, as You do, that the sun is warm; tell me that You have given me life. I know that You know all things. You know that I love You. I may infer, therefore, that I know I am loved by You! So, let me come to You in the confidence of Your love. I long to be nearer, in the clearer sight, the fuller sense and more joyful awareness of Your love forever. Father, into Your hand I commend my spirit. Lord Jesus, receive my spirit. Amen.

RICHARD BAXTER

8 July

O merciful God, fill our hearts, we pray Thee, with the graces of Thy Holy Spirit – with love, joy, peace, long-suffering, gentleness, goodness, faith, meekness, temperance. Teach us to love those who hate us; to pray for those who despitefully use us; that we may be the children of Thee, our Father, who makest Thy sun to shine on the evil and on the good, and sendest rain on the just and on the unjust.

In adversity, grant us grace to be patient; in prosperity, keep us humble; may we guard the door of our lips: may we lightly esteem the pleasures of the world, and thirst after heavenly things, O Lord, Thou Judge of all.

ANSELM

9 July

Thou, O our Father, art the Guardian and Defender of all who trust in Thee. Without Thy protection we can find no safety; without Thy Almighty power we cannot resist the might of those who seek to do us harm. Thou art God, and there is none beside Thee; Thou art great and doest wondrous things; honour and praise are Thine.

To Thee the lowly in heart, to Thee the souls of the righteous, to Thee angels and archangels, fall down in continual adoration. Help us, O Lord our God, our Life and our Strength, to praise and celebrate Thee, although we be unworthy. Shed abroad Thy love in our hearts; open Thou our lips; may our souls be filled with Thy praise; and our tongues sing of Thy glory.

ST AUGUSTINE

10 July

God of all goodness, grant us to desire ardently, to seek wisely, to know surely, and to accomplish perfectly thy holy will, for the glory of thy name. Amen.

ST THOMAS AQUINAS

O Lord of all good life, we pray Thee to purify our lives. Help us each day to know more of Thee, and by the power of Thy Spirit use us to shew forth Thyself to others. Make us humble, brave and loving; make us ready for adventure. We do not ask that Thou wilt keep us safe, but keep us ever loyal to the example of our Lord and Saviour, Jesus Christ. Amen.

SCRIPTURE UNION PRAYERS FOR SCHOOLS, YOUTH GROUPS, CHURCH SERVICES AND PERSONAL USE

11 July

Merciful Lord,
Long-suffering and full of pity,
light which never sets.
God is the Lord who hath shewed us light.
O by Thy resurrection raise us up
unto newness of life,
supplying to us frames of repentance.
The God of peace,
who did bring again from the dead
the great Shepherd of the sheep,
through the blood of the everlasting covenant,
our Lord Jesus Christ,
perfect us in every good work,
to do His will,
working in us what is acceptable before Him,
through Jesus Christ,
to whom be glory for ever.

LANCELOT ANDREWES

12 July

Our Gracious God
open our eyes
to the greatness of your love
for the world you have created.
Renew us by your Spirit
that we may share your good news
  of hope and new life
  of justice and peace
  of compassion and forgiveness.
Revive your Church and save your people.

JOHN PERRY

Lord of every thought and action,
  Lord to send and Lord to stay,
Lord in speaking, writing, giving,
  Lord in all things to obey;
  Lord of all there is of me,
  Now and evermore to be.

ALAN REDPATH

13 July

May God the Father and the Eternal High Priest, Jesus Christ, build us up in faith and truth and chastity, and grant to us our portion among the saints with all those who believe on our Lord Jesus Christ. We pray for all saints; for kings and rulers; for our persecutors and for enemies of the Cross; and for ourselves we pray that our fruit may abound and we may be made perfect in Christ Jesus our Lord.

POLYCARP

Lord Jesus, thank You that You are always with me and that, when I look up, I see You. Everything else becomes small, compared to this joy.

CORRIE TEN BOOM

14 July

Whom have we, Lord, like you –
The Great One who became small, the Wakeful who slept,
The Pure One who was baptised, the Living One who died,
The King who abased himself to ensure honour for all?
Blessed is your honour!
It is right that man should acknowledge your divinity,
It is right for heavenly beings to worship your humanity.
The heavenly beings were amazed to see how small you
became,
And earthly ones to see how exalted.

EPHREM THE SYRIAN

15 July

Lord Jesus Christ
You said

May they all be one, just as, Father,
You are in me and I am in You,
So that the world may believe
It was You who sent me.

Dear Lord, bring together in love and
peace all who believe in You.

Amen.

BASIL HUME

All shall be Amen and Alleluia.
We shall rest and we shall see.
We shall see and we shall know.
We shall know and we shall love.
We shall love and we shall praise.
Behold our end which is no end.

ST AUGUSTINE

16 July

To thee, O God, I give myself entirely all the days of my
    life:
my understanding; my only care to know thee,
my will; to will whatsoever thou willest, and that only,
my affections; what thou lovest may I love; what thou hatest
    may I hate,
my body; to glorify thee with it, preserving it fit for thee to
    dwell in,
my worldly goods; using them only for thee.

I give thee myself, my reputation and my all. Be thou my
    portion and my all.

O God, when hereafter I shall be tempted to break this sol-
    emn engagement, may my answer be 'I am not my own
    but for my God.'
God be merciful to me, a sinner.
Amen.

JOHN WESLEY

17 July

O Lord, give Thy blessing, we pray Thee, to our daily work, that we may do it in faith and heartily, as to the Lord and not unto men. All our powers of body and mind are Thine, and we would devote them to Thy service.

Do Thou, O Lord, so bless our efforts that they may bring forth in us the fruits of true wisdom. Teach us to seek after truth and enable us to gain it; but grant that we may ever speak the truth in love; that, while we know earthly things, we may know Thee, and be known by Thee, through and in Thy Son Jesus Christ. Give us this day Thy Holy Spirit, that we may be Thine in body and spirit in all our work and all our refreshments; through Jesus Christ, Thy Son, our Lord. Amen.

THOMAS ARNOLD

18 July

Father, here is a new day. I take it as a present from you. I know it has come with no strings attached, but I want to arrive at the end of it knowing that you're pleased because I have enjoyed it properly and haven't neglected it, broken it, misused it, abused it, wasted it or spoiled this gift. So I ask that I may be filled with your Spirit right now at the start so that, being filled with your love for Jesus, I too may love him with the same love as is in you and serve him by washing the feet of his disciples and blessing my neighbours. In his name, Amen.

ROGER FORSTER

19 July

Dear Father, I worship you because you are so great and good. You are in charge of the whole world and yet you care about me.

Thank you for loving me – thank you for sending Jesus to save me. I am grateful that you don't sleep, for when I can't sleep I can talk with you.

Lord, I long to be physically healed, to walk, to run and dance. I know you are a healing God. I know that your plan for me is that I should become like Jesus and that you use everything – even disability – to perfect this. But I don't want to miss anything that Jesus died to gain for us. So I am asking that your purposes for me will be fulfilled.

I do want to glorify you through (my) Christlikeness in my life – but I also want the world to see your healing power, so, please Lord, keep working on me by your Holy Spirit, and let me see answers to my prayer.

PEGGY BUCHANAN

20 July

In mercy, O Lord, pardon all that Thy pure and holy eyes have seen amiss in us this day, in our thoughts or desires, our words or actions ... Enter not into judgement with Thy servants ... but, pardon all our sins, negligences, and ignorances for the sake of Him Who ever liveth to make intercession for us, our Mediator and Advocate Jesus Christ.

For the unspeakable gift of Thy dear Son; for the blessings of this life; for the expectation of the life to come; all glory, thanks, and praise be given unto Thee, O Father Almighty, Who with the Son, and Holy Spirit lives and reignest, ever one God, world without end. Amen.

BENJAMIN JENKS

21 July

O God, who art light, and in whom is no darkness at all, shine into our hearts by Thy Holy Spirit, and cause us, in Thy light, clearly to see light.

Deliver us from ignorance, error, and unbelief; help us, as children of light and of the day, to renounce the hidden things of dishonesty, and to have no fellowship with the works of darkness; enable us to walk in truth and uprightness, in purity and sincerity, before Thee, that our fellowship may be with Thee, the Father, and with Thy Son, Jesus Christ; and that, when the shadows of this life have passed away, we may enjoy the vision of Thy heavenly glory, and may ourselves shine forth, with the brightness of the sun, in Thy kingdom for ever and ever.

PRAYERS FOR SOCIAL AND FAMILY WORSHIP
(*by the Church of Scotland*)

22 July

I do not ask, O Lord, that life may be
       A pleasant road;
I do not ask that Thou wouldst take from me
       Aught of its load;
I do not ask that flowers should always spring
       Beneath my feet;
I know too well the poison and the sting
       Of things too sweet.
For one thing only, Lord, dear Lord, I plead,
       Lead me aright –
Though strength should falter, and though heart
       should bleed –
       Through Peace to Light.
I do not ask, O Lord, that Thou shouldst shed
       Full radiance here;
Give but a ray of peace, that I may tread
       Without fear.
I do not ask my cross to understand,
       My way to see –
Better in darkness just to feel Thy hand
       And follow Thee.
Joy is like restless day; but peace divine
       Like quiet night:
Lead me, O Lord – till perfect Day shall shine,
       Through Peace to Light.

ADELAIDE ANNE PROCTER

23 July

Glory be to God on high, and in earth peace, goodwill towards men. We praise Thee, we bless Thee, we worship Thee, we glorify Thee, we give thanks to Thee for Thy great glory, O Lord God, heavenly King, God the Father Almighty.

O Lord, the only-begotten Son Jesus Christ; O Lord God, Lamb of God, Son of the Father, that takest away the sins of the world, have mercy upon us. Thou that takest away the sins of the world receive our prayer. Thou that sittest at the right hand of God the Father, have mercy upon us.

For Thou only art holy; Thou only art the Lord; Thou only, O Christ, with the Holy Ghost, art most high in the glory of God the Father. Amen.

BOOK OF COMMON PRAYER

24 July

Lord,
Help me to live this day
Quietly, easily.
Help me to lean upon Thy
Great strength
Trustfully, restfully,
To wait for the unfolding
Of Thy will
Patiently, serenely,
To meet others
Peacefully, joyously,
To face tomorrow
Confidently, courageously.
Amen.

ST FRANCIS OF ASSISI

O God, the might of all them that put their trust in thee,
grant that we may be more than conquerors over all things
that make war upon our souls, that at the last we may enter
into the perfect peace of thy presence through Jesus Christ
our Lord. Amen.

ROMAN BREVIARY

25 July

Our God, we come to Thee by Jesus Christ who has gone within the veil on our behalf and ever liveth to make intercession for us. Our poor prayers could never reach Thee were it not for Him, but His hands are full of sweet perfume which makes our pleading sweet with Thee. His blood is sprinkled on the mercy seat, and now we know that Thou dost always hear those who approach Thee through that ever blessed name.

We pray now because we have been quickened; we have received a new life, and the breath of that life is prayer. We have risen from the dead, and we also make intercession through the life which Christ has given us. We plead with the living God with living hearts because He has made us to live.

C. H. SPURGEON

26 July

Lord Jesus Christ,
All that I remember of you
comes from a single source –
the living holy Scriptures,
written down
to convey truth and life to all.

Thank you, Lord,
for those faithful men
who witnessed and suffered for it.
Thank you for this gospel of salvation,
the good news of God.

Make me a better student of your Word:
a workman, labouring;
a tradesman, experienced;
a craftsman, skilled.
A better listener,
a better discerner, and
a better witness too.

I know that spiritual power
lies not in printed words
but in yourself, your Holy Spirit.
May he teach me the truth
and touch with power
my springs of thought and action.
For your Name's sake.
Amen.

TIMOTHY DUDLEY-SMITH

27 July

O Eternal Light, shine into our hearts; eternal Goodness, deliver us from evil, eternal Power, be thou our support, eternal Wisdom, scatter our ignorance, eternal Pity, have mercy upon us. Grant that with all our heart and mind and soul and strength we may seek thy face, and finally bring us, by thine infinite mercy, to thy holy presence, through Jesus Christ our Lord. Amen.

ALCUIN

Refresh our bodies, we pray Thee, with quiet and comfortable rest; but especially let our souls be refreshed with Thy love.

We humbly pray Thee, for Christ's sake.

MATTHEW HENRY

28 July

Almighty God, who hast given us a land wherein we are free to read and hear Thy word, to confess Thy name, and to labour together for the extension of Thy kingdom: grant, we ask Thee, that the liberty we enjoy may be continued to our children, and our children's children; and that the power of the gospel may here abound to the blessing of all the nations of the earth, and to Thine eternal glory; through Jesus Christ our Lord. Amen.

LUTHERAN SERVICE BOOK

29 July

Our Father, unto Thee in the light of our Saviour's blessed Life, we would lift our souls. We thank Thee for that true Light shining in our world with still increasing brightness. We thank Thee for all who have walked therein, and especially for those near to us and dear, in whose lives we have seen this excellent glory and beauty. May we know that when these earthly days come to an end, it is not that our service of Thee and of one another may cease, but that it may begin anew. Make us glad in all who have faithfully lived; make us glad in all who have peacefully died. Lift us into light and love and purity and blessedness, and give us at last our portion with those who have trusted in Thee and sought, in small things as in great, in things temporal and things eternal, to do Thy Holy Will. Amen.

RUFUS ELLIS

30 July

Deep in my heart there is a sigh,
    A longing, Lord, for Thee;
To know the depths that in Thee lie,
    The grace of Calvary.
O grant that I might understand
    Thy glorious mystery,
More of Thyself, and by Thy hand
    Obedience stir in me.
Thy living power I long to prove
    In resurrection might,
With overcoming grace to move
    Each sin that dims this light.
O grant that I may find the source
    Of hidden strength and stay,
Which flows from Thee, and on its course
    O draw my soul each day.

VERNON HIGHAM

31 July

O God, the strength of all them that put their trust in thee, mercifully accept our prayers; and because through the weakness of our mortal nature we can do no good thing without thee, grant us the help of thy grace, that in keeping of thy commandments we may please thee, both in will and deed, through Jesus Christ our Lord. Amen.

BOOK OF COMMON PRAYER

I should never do anything if you left it to me to do it. It is yours to prevent me from falling and to set right that which is not well.

BROTHER LAWRENCE

1 August

Keep me in Thy love
As Thou wouldst that all should be kept in mine.
May everything in this my being be directed to Thy glory
And may I never despair
For I am under Thy hand
And in Thee is all power and goodness.

DAG HAMMARSKJÖLD

Lead us, Father, along the paths You choose for us, whatever they may be. Help us to realise every day that You do not slumber or sleep and that You will not let our feet slip. We thank You for Your wisdom in leading us.

CORRIE TEN BOOM

2 August

Lord, grant me time enough to do all the chores,
Join in the games,
Help with the lessons,
Say the night prayers,
And still have a few moments left for me.

Lord, grant me energy enough to be
Bread baker and bread winner,
Knee patcher and peace maker,
Ball player and bill juggler.

Lord, grant me hands enough to
Wipe away the tears,
Reach out when I'm needed,
Hug and to hold. To tickle and touch.

Lord, grant me heart enough to
Share and to care,
Listen and to understand,
And to make a loving home for my family.

A SINGLE PARENT'S PRAYER
(*anonymous*)

3 August

O God, Who has commanded us to be perfect, as Thou our Father in heaven art perfect: put into our hearts, we pray Thee, a continual desire to obey Thy holy will. Teach us day by day what Thou wouldest have us do, and give us grace and power to fulfil the same. May we never from love of ease, decline the path which Thou pointest out, nor, for fear of shame, turn away from it. Amen.

HENRY ALFORD

Our Father, teach us not only Thy will, but how to do it. Teach us the best way of doing the best thing, lest we spoil the end by unworthy means.

J. H. JOWETT

4 August

O Lord our God, the Father of Our Lord Jesus Christ of Whom He is the very image, I look to Thee and make my prayer. Bless me this hour with the feeling of Thy presence and the glow of Thy nearness, for I do trust Thee and hope only in Thee. In much and growing praise to Thee, O Lord, I look up. Kindle in me the sacred fire till I am glowing with fire divine. Oh by Thy indwelling Spirit knit me together into worship and beauty and holiness. Lord, touch my body and spirit till both are sweeping in one with Thee.

OSWALD CHAMBERS

5 August

Father God, thank You for Your great mercy and grace. Your powerful presence calls out to us.

Thank You for the blood of Jesus Christ and the Holy Spirit moving among us, for bringing us here today to hear Your message and experience Your great miraculous power. O Living God, help us to come before You with open hearts to acknowledge and trust Your Holy Spirit and hear Your call to repent. O Jesus Christ our Saviour, You shed Your blood to save us who deserved eternal death. We know that Your blood can lead us to great victorious living. Your blood can heal us and offer eternal peace to us. Thank You for so great a salvation. Amen.

DAVID YONGGI CHO

6 August

O Lord God Almighty, eternal and omnipresent God, blessed for ever, we commit unto Thee, for this day, and our whole lives, our bodies and our souls, our thoughts and affections, our words and actions; beseeching Thee to take care of us, and to guard us from the dangers and temptations which continually beset us; from all evil, and especially from sin.

Teach us to do the thing that pleaseth Thee, for Thou art our God. Give us a right judgement of all things, that we may ask such things as Thou delightest to give and such as are best for us to receive. Put away from us all hurtful things, and give us such things as are profitable for us. O Thou blessed Physician, we pray Thee to heal the wounds of our souls. Put Thy fear into our hearts, that we may not depart from Thee.

ST AUGUSTINE

7 August

Hear us, O never-failing Light, Lord our God, the Fountain of light, the Light of Thine Angels, Principalities, Powers, and of all intelligent beings; Who hast created the light of Thy Saints. May our souls be lamps of Thine, kindled and illuminated by Thee. May they shine and burn with the truth, and never go out in darkness and ashes. May the gloom of sins be cleared away, and the light of perpetual faith abide with us. Amen.

MOZARABIC LITURGY

Deliver each of us from the sins which most easily beset us. O Lord, grant that Thy good Spirit may this day abide within us; and dispose us to every good work.

HENRY THORNTON

8 August

Eternal God, since we know not what a day may bring forth, but only that the hour for serving Thee is always present, may we wake to the instant claims of Thy holy will, not waiting for tomorrow, but yielding today. Consecrate with Thy presence the way our feet may go, and the humblest work will shine, and the roughest places be made plain. Lift us above unrighteous anger and mistrust into faith and hope and charity by a simple and steadfast reliance on Thy sure will. In all things draw us to the mind of Christ, that Thy lost image may be traced again, and that Thou mayest own us as at one with Him and Thee, to the glory of Thy great Name. Amen.

BOOK OF CONGREGATIONAL PRAYER, 1920

9 August

May I speak each day according to Thy justice,
Each day may I show Thy chastening, O God;
May I speak each day according to Thy wisdom,
Each day and night may I be at peace with Thee.

Each day may I count the causes of Thy mercy,
May I each day give heed to Thy laws;
Each day may I compose to Thee a song,
May I harp each day Thy praise, O God.

May I each day give love to Thee, Jesus,
Each night may I do the same,
Each day and night, dark and light,
May I laud Thy goodness to me, O God.

CARMINA GADELICA

10 August

O Lord, may we feel that Thy love which is now, ever shall be; this robe of the flesh is Thy gift to Thy child, and, when it is worn out, Thou wilt clothe him again; this work of life is the work Thou hast given us to do, and, when it is done, Thou wilt give us more; this love, that makes all our life so glad, flows from Thee, for Thou art Love, and we shall love forever. Help us to feel how, day by day, we see some dim shadow of the eternal day that will break upon us at the last. May the Gospel of Thy Son, the whisper of Thy Spirit, unite to make our faith in the life to come, strong and clear; then shall we be glad when Thou shalt call us, and enter into thy glory in Jesus Christ. Amen.

ROBERT COLLYER

11 August

O my God where art Thou? Come, come; I am ready to lay down my life for Thy Truth patiently as a lamb. It is the cause of justice – it is Thine. I will never separate myself from Thee, neither now nor through Eternity. And though the world should be filled with devils, though my body, the work of Thy hands, should be slain, stretched upon the pavement, be cut to pieces and reduced to ashes, my soul is Thine. Yes! Thy Word is my assurance of it, that my soul shall abide forever with Thee. O God help me! Amen.

MARTIN LUTHER

12 August

O God, you are my Creator, and I am your creature
You are so great and I am so tiny and insignificant
You are Holy and right, and I am all wrong and confused.
Oh Lord Jesus, I don't understand it, but with all my heart I
believe that on the cross you bled and died for me.
I also believe that you rose again and live today.
Although my mind can't grasp all this yet,
I want to come to you now,
With my ignorance – please teach me
With my sin – please forgive and cleanse me
With my unbelief – please give me faith
With my weakness – please give me your strength
With my evil heart – please give me your purity
With my blindness – please give me sight
With my darkness – please give me your light.
Come into my heart – please make me a Christian.
Amen.

TOM REES
(*prayer that was prayed by him at the end of an
evangelistic rally in the Royal Albert Hall,
London, 1950*)

13 August

He whom none may touch is seized;
He who looses Adam from the curse is bound.
He who tries the hearts and inner thoughts of man
    is unjustly brought to trial;
He who closed the abyss is shut in prison.
He before whom the powers of heaven stand with
    trembling stands before Pilate;
The Creator is struck by the hand of his creature.
He who comes to judge the living and the dead is
    condemned to the Cross;
The Destroyer of hell is enclosed in a tomb.
O thou who dost endure all these things in thy
    tender love,
Who hast saved all men from the curse,
O long-suffering Lord, glory to thee.

AN ORTHODOX PRAYER

14 August

Open Thou my heart for Thy love, keep Thy love in me, prepare me by Thy love for greater fullness of Thy love, until I have reached the fullest measure of love, which Thou, in Thine eternal love, hast willed for me. Make me, in thought, word, and deed, to love Thee, and thank Thee, and praise Thee, and praising Thee to love Thee more, and know Thee more, how worthy Thou art of all love and praise, until I be fitted with all Thy saints and angels to love Thee and praise Thee everlastingly, and breathe out my soul to Thee in loving Thee and praising Thee for all Thy boundless, undeserved love to me, Thy poor sinner, yet, though a sinner, Thine, O God my God. Amen.

E. B. PUSEY

15 August

May we realise how open and clear Thou hast made the way to the footstool of Thy Throne of Grace.

Bless our fellow Christians everywhere. Thou seest them scattered over the wide earth: some alone, others in large numbers. Wherever they are, there be Thou, Thou their helper, that they may not want. Hear the secret intercessions of Thy Church.

Be Thou the end of life to us, be Thou the source and spring of life, be Thou all in all to us.

Attract us strongly that we may live near Thee. May our ends, objects, and desires be as Thine own. This is a gloriously high aim, but we can attain to it if Thou dost lift us up. Raise us by Thy Holy Spirit now.

SAMUEL MARTIN

16 August

We pray, our Father, for those whose freedom has been taken from them:

for all who suffer imprisonment, whether for crime or for conscience sake;

for all whose vision of your world is seen through bars, and in whose heart the lamp of hope burns low.

God of mercy, give them help according to their need, and hear our prayer for Jesus Christ's sake.

TIMOTHY DUDLEY-SMITH

Our days are numbered: let us spare
Our anxious hearts needless care:
'Tis Thine to number out our days;
'Tis ours to give them to Thy praise.

MADAME JEANNE GUYON

17 August

Heavenly Father, give us such a fresh picture of Your heaven and all that awaits us up ahead. Help us to look into Your beautiful eyes and be calmed by Your grace and peace. Thank You for Your unconditional love and forgiveness whatever happens. Be patient with me when I don't exhibit the evidences of a son greatly loved; embraced by You, made clean, given new clothes, a ring, sandals and a celebratory meal. Thank You for bathing me in Your love. I love You very much. Amen.

LYNDON BOWRING

18 August

O Thou, who in almighty power was meek, and in perfect excellency was lowly, grant unto us the same mind, that we may acknowledge our weakness, and may mourn over our evil will. Our bodies are frail and fading; our minds are blind and froward; all that we have which is our own, is naught; if we have any good thing in us, it is wholly Thy gift. O Saviour, since Thou, the Lord of heaven and earth, didst humble Thyself, grant unto us true humility, and make us like Thyself. And then, of Thine infinite goodness, raise us to Thine everlasting glory, who livest and reignest with the Father, and the Holy Ghost, for ever and ever. Amen.

THOMAS CRANMER

19 August

O Spirit of God we love Thee this day, especially for dwelling in us.

O Lord we would delight ourselves in Thee this day. Give us faith and love and hope that with these three graces we may draw very near to the Triune God. Thou wilt keep us, Thou wilt preserve us, Thou wilt feed us, Thou wilt lead us, and Thou wilt bring us to the mind of God, and there wilt Thou show us Thy love, and in the glory everlasting and boundless, there wilt Thou make us know and taste and feel the joys that cannot be expressed.

We also bless Thee, O God, as the God of our redemption, for Thou hast so loved us as to give even Thy dear Son for us.

C. H. SPURGEON

20 August

Lord Jesus Christ,
Thou wast poor, and in misery,
    a captive and forsaken as I am.
Thou knowest all man's distress;
Thou abidest with me when all others have deserted me;
Thou wilt not forget me, Thou seekest me.
Thou willest that I should know Thee and turn to Thee.
Lord, I hear Thy call and follow Thee;
    do Thou help me.
Lord, whatsoever this day may bring,
    Thy name be praised.
Be gracious unto me and help me.
Grant me strength to bear whatsoever Thou dost send,
    and let not fear overrule me.
I trust Thy grace, and commit my life wholly into Thy
    hands.
Whether I live or whether I die, I am with Thee,
    and Thou art with me,
        O my Lord and my God.
Lord, I wait for Thy salvation,
    and for the coming of Thy Kingdom. Amen.

DIETRICH BONHOEFFER

21 August

Eternal God whose Word dispels the ambiguities of human existence, remind us, we pray, that time and life are divinely entrusted to us to find salvation and joy in you.

Were you not this planet's Creator and Sustainer it would surely move toward ignominious annihilation. Thank you, God, that scientific genius with its big bangs will not have the last word. We glory therefore and instead in the reality of your unfailing wisdom, and in the loving gift of your Son to explain the beginning and ongoing course of life.

Great God, our Maker, Sustainer, Redeemer and King of kings, so indwell our minds, hearts and bodies, we pray, that we daily manifest and represent you in word, life and deed to your glory and the extension of your Kingdom. This we pray in Jesus' Name. Amen.

CARL F. H. HENRY

22 August

God, send us a Revival that will turn the people of God back from their worldliness and idols to serve the true and living God – back from 'broken cisterns' to the 'Fountain of living waters'.

A Revival that will save the people of God from covetousness and love of the world and all uncleanness of spirit, mind and body.

Yes! A Revival that will never need to be revived! But will sweep on like a mighty wave of the sea that nothing can hinder, until time shall be no more!

For such a Revival, O God, we pray.

A PRAYER FOR REVIVAL (PART TWO)

23 August

This is the world
You loved so much that for it
You gave your only begotten
Son, our Lord and Saviour Jesus Christ, to hang
From the cross, done to death
Love nearly overwhelmed by hate
Light nearly extinguished by darkness
Life nearly destroyed by death –
But not quite –

For love vanquished hate
For life overcame death, there –
Light overwhelmed
Darkness, there –
And we can live with hope.
For peace,
For transfiguration, for compassion,
                    for soldiers,
For civilians, for peace, for Shalom,
For family, for togetherness –

O my God, our God, O my Father
When will we ever learn?
When will they ever learn?

DESMOND TUTU

24 August

Blessed art Thou, Lord, God of Israel,
our Father,
from everlasting to everlasting.
Thine, O Lord,
is the greatness and the power,
the triumph and the victory,
the praise and the strength,
for Thou rulest over all
in heaven and on earth.
At Thy face every king is troubled,
and every nation.
Thine, O Lord, is the kingdom
and the supremacy over all,
and over all rule.
With Thee is wealth, and glory is from
Thy countenance;
Thou rulest over all, O Lord,
the Ruler of all rule;
and in Thine hand is strength and power,
and in Thine hand to give to all things
greatness and strength.
And now, Lord, we confess to Thee,
and we praise Thy glorious Name.

LANCELOT ANDREWES

25 August

Almighty God, we bless and praise Thee that we have wakened to the light of another earthly day; and now we will think of what a day should be. Our days are Thine, let them be spent for Thee. Our days are few, let them be spent with care. There are dark days behind us, forgive their sinfulness; there may be dark days before us, strengthen us for their trials. We pray Thee to shine on this day, the day which we may call our own. Lord, we go to our daily work, help us to take pleasure therein. Show us clearly what our duty is, help us to be faithful in doing it. Let all we do be well done, fit for Thine eye to see. Give us strength to do, patience to bear, let our courage never fail. When we cannot love our work, let us think of it as Thy task, and by our true love to Thee make unlovely things shine in the light of Thy great love; through Jesus Christ our Lord. Amen.

GEORGE DAWSON

26 August

O God Whose kingdom is righteousness, and peace and joy in the Holy Ghost, grant us the peace of knowing and loving Thee; the perfect peace of those whose minds are stayed on Thee, the peace which passeth all understanding.

O Prince of Peace, may Thy kingdom be more and more established in the earth. Hasten the time when men shall beat their swords into ploughshares, and their spears into pruning hooks, when nation shall not lift up sword against nation, neither learn war any more: O Lord, revive Thy work: Hasten the time when the earth shall be filled with the knowledge of God as the waters cover the sea. Amen.

THOMAS HALL

27 August

Heavenly Father, who hast given us in thy Son an High Priest who, partaking of our nature and consecrating himself on our behalf, has offered himself in sacrifice for our sins once for all upon the Cross. We thank thee that now he presents us in himself before thee as those whom he has brothered and redeemed; receive us as we come before thee in his name, mercifully absolve us from our sins and cleanse us from every stain.

THOMAS TORRANCE

O Eternal God, Thou Fountain of justice, mercy and benediction, be pleased to let Thy Holy Spirit be for ever present with me, so that I may be diligent, just, and faithful.

JEREMY TAYLOR

28 August

God of all grace, enable us this day, and all the days of our sojourning in the body, to live by faith in the Son of God, who loved us, and gave Himself for us. Give us grace continually to abide in Him, that we may bear much fruit. And whatsoever we do, in word or deed, dispose us to do all in the name of the Lord Jesus, giving thanks to God, even the Father, by Him.

PRAYERS FOR SOCIAL AND FAMILY WORSHIP
(by the Church of Scotland)

Help me, Lord, to live one day at a time. Thank You that Your grace is sufficient for today and that I don't need to worry about tomorrow, because Your grace will be sufficient for tomorrow also.

CORRIE TEN BOOM

29 August

O God, we confess that we have sinned against Thee in thought, word, and deed; we have not loved Thee with all our heart and soul and mind and strength; we have not loved our neighbours as ourselves. Have mercy upon us, forgive our sins, cleanse us from every kind of wrong, and help us to overcome our faults; through Jesus Christ our Lord. Amen.

SCRIPTURE UNION PRAYERS FOR SCHOOLS,
YOUTH GROUPS, CHURCH SERVICES AND
PERSONAL USE

Grant, O Lord, that we, remembering how thou hast mercifully pardoned our misdeeds, may frankly forgive all those who trespass against us, and may maintain constant peace among ourselves and all men ... Grant this, O heavenly Father, for Thy dear Son's sake, Jesus Christ our Lord. Amen.

DESIDERIUS ERASMUS

30 August

O Word of our God, I betrayed you, the Truth, with my falsehood, when I promised to hallow the hours that vanish away.

In overtaking me, night does not find me undarkened by sin. I did indeed pray, and I thought to stand blameless at eve.

But someway and somewhere my feet have stumbled and fallen; for a storm-cloud swooped on me, envious lest I be saved.

Kindle for me your light, O Christ, restore me by your Presence.

GREGORY OF NAZIANZUS

Lord Jesus, I am longing
From sin to be set free:
To find my deep desiring
Forever fixed on Thee.
All hope I now abandon
Myself to conquer sin;
Invade my willing nature
And come and dwell within.

W. E. SANGSTER

31 August

I need thee to teach me day by day, according to each day's opportunities and needs. Give me, O my Lord, that purity of conscience which alone can receive, which alone can improve Thy inspirations.

My ears are dull, so that I cannot hear Thy voice. My eyes are dim, so that I cannot see Thy tokens. Thou alone canst quicken my hearing, and purge my sight, and cleanse and renew my heart.

Teach me to sit at Thy feet, and to hear Thy word.

JOHN HENRY NEWMAN

Fix Thou our steps, O Lord, that we stagger not at the uneven motions of the world, but steadily go on to our glorious home; not turning out of the way for anything that befalls us.

JOHN WESLEY

1 September

Lord,
because you prayed
that we would all be one,
renew your mind in ours
so that we will yearn for the unity you seek.

Unite our hearts,
that we may find
a place for others in our plans.

Unite us with a vision of a world
in search of you.

Enclose us in your purpose
to bring all peoples to a knowledge of your love.
Bring us together to bring hope
to our neighbours in despair.

Make us one Lord,
so that together
we may look much more like you.

JOEL EDWARDS

2 September

O Loving Father, grant unto us, when the ways of life seem hard and the brightness of life is gone, the wisdom that deepens faith when sight is dim. And whensoever Thy ways, in nature or in the soul, are hard to understand, then may our great confidence, our boundless trust, our living faith in Thee be great; and as children knowing they are loved, cared for, guarded, kept, may we with a quiet mind at all times put our trust in the unseen God; so may we face life here without fear and whatsoever is in the life to come. Give us confidence and trust in Thee, both now and evermore. Amen.

GEORGE DAWSON

3 September

O God, we have known and believed the love that Thou hast for us. May we, by dwelling in love, dwell in Thee, and Thou in us. May we learn to love Thee Whom we have not seen, by loving our brethren whom we have seen. Teach us, O heavenly Father, the love wherewith Thou hast loved us; fashion us, O blessed Lord, after Thine own example of love; shed abroad, O Thou Holy Spirit of Love, the love of God and man in our hearts. Amen.

HENRY ALFORD

Blessed Lord, I beseech Thee to pour down upon me such grace as may not only cleanse this life of mine, but beautify it a little, if it be Thy will.

JAMES SKINNER

4 September

Hold Thou my hand: and closer, closer draw me
To Thy dear self, my hope, my joy, my all;
Hold Thou my hand: lest haply I should wander,
And missing Thee, my trembling feet should fall.

Hold Thou my hand: so weak I am, and helpless;
I dare not take one step without Thy aid.
Hold Thou my hand: for then, O loving Saviour
No dread of ill shall make my soul afraid.

FANNY CROSBY
(two verses from one of her hymns)

Help us, Lord, to make a clean cut with everything we
know is wrong. Thank You, that Your Spirit in us causes us
to feel uneasy about all we have to put away.

CORRIE TEN BOOM

5 September

Most holy, blessed, and glorious Lord God, whose we are, and whom we are bound to serve, we are not our own, but Thine, and unto Thee do we lift up our souls.

Thou givest unto all life, and breath, and all things. Thou hast fed us, and kept us all our life long, unto this day. One day telleth another, and one night certifieth another, that Thou art good and doest good, and never failest those that seek Thee.

Do for us, we pray Thee, abundantly above that we are able to ask or think, for the sake of our Lord and Saviour Jesus Christ, to whom, with the Father and the Eternal Spirit, be all honour, praise, and glory, now and for ever. Amen.

MATTHEW HENRY

6 September

Grant, O Lord, favourable weather, peaceful showers, beneficent dews, abundance of fruits, and to crown the year with Thy goodness: for the eyes of all wait upon Thee, and Thou givest them their meat in due season: thou openest Thy hand and fillest all things living with gladness.

Remember, O Lord, all who bring forth fruit, and labour honourably in the services of Thy Church, and all those who remember the poor, the widows, the orphans, the strangers, the needy, and all who have desired us to remember them in our prayers.

LITURGY OF ST JAMES

7 September

Arm me, O Thou God of battles, with courage this day, that I may not fall before my enemies. To quarrel is Thine, let the victory be Thine. Tie to my sinews the strength of David, that I may with a pebble stone strike to the earth these giants that fight against Thy truth. So let me fight that, whether I come off lame or sound, dead or alive, I may live or die Thy soldier.

THOMAS DEKKER

Lord God, remind me always,
Let nothing disturb thee,
Nothing affright thee;
All things are passing:
God never changeth:
Patient endurance
Attaineth to all things:
Who God possesseth
In nothing is wanting.
Alone God sufficeth.

ST TERESA OF AVILA

8 September

The Lord hath granted His loving-kindness
in the day time;
and in the night season did I sing of Him,
and made my prayer unto the God of my life.
As long as I live will I magnify Thee on this manner,
And lift up my hands in Thy Name.
Let my prayer be set forth in Thy sight
as the incense,
and let the lifting up of my hands
be an evening sacrifice.
Blessed art Thou, O Lord, our God.

LANCELOT ANDREWES

Holy Father, make us holy.
Holy Jesus, make us holy.
Holy Spirit, make us holy.
Holy God, make us whole. Amen.

A PRAYER FROM THE INSTITUTE
FOR SPIRITUALITY, CPSA

9 September

O God, Thou art Life, Wisdom, Truth, Bounty, and Blessedness, the Eternal, the only true Good. My God and my Lord, Thou art my hope and my heart's joy.

Lord, make me to know Thee aright, that I may more and more love, enjoy, and possess Thee. And since, in the life here below, I cannot fully attain this blessedness, let it at least grow in me day by day, until it all be fulfilled at last in the life to come.

Here be the knowledge of Thee increased, and there let it be perfected. Here let my love to Thee grow, and there let it ripen; that my joy being here great in hope, may there in fruition be made perfect.

ANSELM

10 September

If only
If only I hadn't
If only I could still
If only he was here
If only I had more

Collecting these 'if onlys' has become compulsive, and I can't seem to stop: there are so many of them. They weigh me down and I'm too tired to carry them any longer.

Can I give all these 'if onlys' to you, Lord? Whenever I manage to give you my worthless things, you always give me something far better in exchange. So in the place of all these 'if onlys' I will receive from you the new life you said you would give me. The way I feel right now, I find it hard to believe a new life is possible, but I receive it from you by faith – and I thank you.

JENNIFER REES LARCOMBE

11 September

O Lord Jesus, the brightness of the eternal glory, and the consolation of contrite and weary souls, refresh us with the light of Thy presence; set our hearts at liberty, and let the light of Thy countenance shine upon our souls. For there is none like Thee, O God, there is none that can do the wonders which Thou doest. Thy Word is very good, O Lord, therefore Thy servants love it. Praise and glory be unto Thee, O Thou Eternal Son of the Father: let our lips, and our souls, and all that is within us, praise and bless Thy holy name, for ever and ever. Amen.

THOMAS À KEMPIS

12 September

Lord, Who knowest all things, and lovest all men better than we know; Thine is might, and wisdom, and love to save us. In all time of need, from all evil, the evil of our time and of our hearts, deliver us, good Lord.

From loneliness and discontented brooding; from wondering what Thou wouldst have us do, deliver us, Lord. Especially from whatever sin besets us, save and deliver us with might, O Lord.

From all bereavement, sorrow, and desertion; from all things that separate us from each other and from our God; from all evils we have prayed against, and from all evils we have not thought of, deliver, O Lord, Thy servants, whose hope is in Thy goodness for ever; through Jesus Christ our Lord. Amen.

ROWLAND WILLIAMS

13 September

Ah Lord! I want to be firmly established in you, so I can
keep your commandments.
Ah Lord! I desire to love you, my God, with all my heart,
mind and strength.
I give all of my love to you.
Ah Lord! You search our hearts and only you know me.
With all my heart and strength I come to love you.
As Mary knelt at your feet and broke the vase of anointing
oil, may you receive my deepest love.

A PRAYER FROM CHINA

I confess, with thanksgiving, that you have made me in
your image, so that I may direct all my thoughts to you, and
love you.

ANSELM

14 September

God, who did teach the hearts of Thy faithful people, by the sending to them the light of Thy Holy Spirit: grant us by the same Spirit to have a right judgement in all things, and evermore to rejoice in His holy comfort; through the merits of Christ Jesus our Saviour.

O Holy Ghost, pour out continually, we beseech Thee, Thy gifts upon us and Thy whole Church, that being cleansed and strengthened by Thy grace and power, we may grow into the perfect stature of the Body of Christ; Who liveth and reigneth with the Father and Thee, O Holy Spirit, one God, world without end. Amen.

BOOK OF CONGREGATIONAL PRAYER, 1920

15 September

O Almighty God, cause us so to embrace the mercy which is offered to us in Thy Gospel, that we may go from strength to strength, till we finally reach that heavenly possession which Thy Son, our Saviour, hath purchased for us.

And since we are in ourselves so frail, and compassed about with infirmity, that even when Thou holdest out Thine hand, we sink in sin without Thy continual help, support us, we pray Thee, by Thine almighty power; that we may go forward in the path of Thy commandments, and obtain the victory over all temptations.

JOHN CALVIN

16 September

O Lord Jesus Christ, who hast promised to come again in like manner as Thou hast ascended into heaven. Keep us ever watchful for Thy glorious appearing. Help us to set our affections on things above, not on things on this earth. May we live as those who wait for their Lord, that when Thou shalt appear we may be made like unto Thee, and see Thee as Thou art; who liveth and reigneth with the Father and the Holy Ghost, ever one God, world without end. Amen.

A. F. THORNHILL

17 September

O God, I desire this day most earnestly to please Thee; to do Thy will in each thing which Thou shalt give me to do; to bear each thing which Thou shalt allow to befall me contrary to my will, meekly, humbly, patiently, as a gift from Thee to subdue self-will in me; and to make Thy will wholly mine. What I do, make me do simply as Thy child; let me be, throughout the day, as a child in his loving father's presence, ever looking up to Thee. May I love Thee for all Thy love. May I thank Thee, if not in words, yet in my heart, for each gift of Thy love, for each comfort which Thou allowest me day by day. Amen.

E. B. PUSEY

18 September

Lord,
in weakness or in strength
we bear your image.
We pray for those we love
who now live in a land of shadows,
where the light of memory is dimmed,
where the familiar lies unknown,
where the beloved become as strangers.
Hold them in your everlasting arms and
grant to those who care

> a strength to serve
> a patience to persevere
> a love to last
> and a peace that passes human understanding.

Hold us in your everlasting arms,
today and for all eternity
through Jesus Christ our Lord.
Amen.

JAMES JONES

19 September

O Lord of Truth

Make your Word
      clear enough to instruct
      rich enough to satisfy
      and
      persuasive enough to redirect our lives

Through Jesus Christ our Lord.

ALEC MOTYER

O Almighty God, may we offer ourselves unto Thee, our souls and bodies, to be a reasonable, true, and lively sacrifice, through Jesus Christ our Lord.

JOHN CALVIN

20 September

O how very right, and fitting, and due,
in all, and for all,
at all times, places, manners,
in every season, every spot,
everywhere, always, altogether,
to remember Thee, to worship Thee,
to confess to Thee, to praise Thee,
to bless Thee, to hymn Thee,
to give thanks to Thee,
Maker, nourisher, guardian, governor,
preserver, worker, perfecter of all.
I commend to Thee, Lord,
my impulses, and my startings,
my intentions, and my attempts,
my going out, and my coming in,
my sitting down, and my rising up.
Thou who didst send down on Thy disciples
Thy Thrice-Holy Spirit,
withdraw not Thou the gift, O Lord, from us,
but renew it in us, day by day,
who ask Thee for it.

LANCELOT ANDREWES

21 September

Saviour, as I read of Thy life on earth, I am impressed by Thy love for men. How Thou didst suffer their weaknesses! How Thou didst so patiently bear with their misunderstanding! And it comforts me to remember that Thou art the same, and that I can find this patient love as truly mine as ever it was theirs. Lord, teach me, for I am ignorant; guide me, lest I stray; impart to me those truths that make for purity and nobility of life. Thou knowest all my sad lapses and broken promises, and, knowing them all, Thou hast, I feel, not lost faith in me; Thou still dost expect me to give Thee my heart's love and best service.

WALTER JAMES

22 September

Lord,
I want to thank you
for your hope bearers
in impossible conditions
of injustice,
distress,
mistreatment,
poverty,
filth
and
depravity –
they shine as lights on the hill.

It is my privilege to meet brothers and sisters worldwide,
who, with a passion that seems to deny the circumstances,
find faith and project strong love
and
are truly your hands, feet, face and smile
to the
refugee, the drug addict, the street kid, the AIDS victim,
the starving village, the elderly, the orphans, the widows.

For 2000 years you have raised them up
to minister, to care, to love unconditionally.
I thank you this is no exclusive club,
no fleeting opportunity to serve,
for we can all be
Jesus
to the poor who, sadly, we always have with us.

DOUG BALFOUR

23 September

Precious Jesus, may we love Thee more, and more manifest our love by deadness to the world. Soon we shall love with purer, stronger love, and rejoice that we were counted worthy to tread in the footsteps of our Forerunner Who is now entered for us within the veil, and ever pleads the sacrifice He once offered for our sins.

JAMES HUDSON TAYLOR

O Father, I praise You that You understand my every sorrow and tear. I acknowledge my insufficiency to handle life's problems in my own strength. I gladly acknowledge my dependence upon You. May Your grace abound to meet my deepest needs. Sustain me as I wait upon You. Fill my heart with Your peace that passes all understanding. Thank You for Your rich provision for me this day. In the name of our Lord Jesus Christ. Amen.

LUIS PALAU

24 September

O Lord, lift up the light of Thy gracious face upon me, and may Thy joy and majesty and grace quicken and lighten and beautify me this day. Grant more grace and tenderness and Christlikeness of spirit.

Lord, this day cause Thy glorious voice to be heard, and heard by me. Oh speak to me, produce Thy stillness, Thy insulating power in my heart and mind, and speak with thrilling power. How essentially I fail without Thee! It is impossible to put into words how I need Thee.

OSWALD CHAMBERS

25 September

O God of love, who hast given us a commandment that we should love one another, even as thou didst love us and give thy beloved Son for our life and salvation: we pray thee give to us thy servants, in all times of our life on the earth, a mind forgetful of past ill-will and a heart to love our brethren; for the sake of Jesus Christ our Lord and only Saviour. Amen.

ST CYRIL

Give us such faith as shall prevail with Thee, being Thine own gift; but give us also an entire submission to Thy holy will. We would wait patiently on Thee, O Lord, until Thou incline Thine ear, and listen to our prayer.

DESIDERIUS ERASMUS

26 September

Lord God Almighty, help me to remember that this life is a schooling time for the eternal home Thou hast prepared for those who love Thee. Keep my eye steadily fixed on that haven of rest and peace, that I may not faint nor be weary from the length of the way, but may strive to walk worthy of my high calling in all meekness and lowliness of heart. And after that I have suffered awhile, when I am strengthened, stablished, settled in Thy love, when I have done all the work Thou hast for me to do, O gracious God, be with me to guide me through the valley of the shadow of death, and, in Thine own good time, take me to dwell with Thee. Amen.

MARIA HARE

27 September

Loving Father in heaven: we thank Thee for the eternal, living, saving word which in Jesus Thou hast spoken and dost still speak to us men. Thou art indeed the first to be concerned with our needs, and Thou art the only one who can fill them. So we can and will lift now our eyes to Thee. Our help cometh from Thee, who hast created heaven and earth.

But now we all stand before Thee, in all our differences, yet alike in that we all are in the wrong with Thee and with one another, that we all must one day die, that we all would be lost without Thy grace.

Do not let us fall, but remain with Thy comfort and also in that Thy grace promised and made available to us all in Thy dear Son, our Lord Jesus Christ. Amen.

KARL BARTH

28 September

Our heavenly Father, we commend to your mercy those for whom life does not spell freedom: prisoners of conscience, the homeless and the handicapped, the sick in body and mind, the elderly who are confined to their homes, those who are enslaved by their passions, and those who are addicted to drugs. Grant that, whatever their outward circumstances, they may find inward freedom, through him who proclaimed release to captives, Jesus Christ our Saviour.

JOHN STOTT

O Lord Jesus Christ, grant that we may be among the number of those who at the last shall bear in their hands the palms of victory, when every knee shall bow before Thee, and every tongue confess that Thou art Lord, to the glory of God the Father. Amen.

SCRIPTURE UNION PRAYERS FOR SCHOOLS,
YOUTH GROUPS, CHURCH SERVICES AND
PERSONAL USE

29 September

Lord Jesus, cause me to know in my daily experience the glory and sweetness of Thy Name, and then teach me how to use it in my prayer, so that I may be even like Israel, a prince prevailing with God. Thy Name is my passport and secures me access; Thy Name is my honour and secures me glory. Blessed Name, Thou art honey in my mouth, music in my ear, heaven in my heart, and all in all to my being.

C. H. SPURGEON

Father, we thank You that we need never walk in darkness, because You are leading us and showing us the way, step by step.

CORRIE TEN BOOM

30 September

O God, renew our spirits by thy Holy Spirit, and draw our hearts this morning unto thyself, that our work may not be a burden, but a delight; and give us such a mighty love to thee as may sweeten all our obedience. Let us not serve with the spirit of bondage as slaves, but with cheerfulness and gladness, as children, delighting ourselves in thee and rejoicing in thy wishes, for the sake of Jesus Christ. Amen.

BENJAMIN JENKS

O Father, light up the small duties of this day's life. May they shine with the beauty of Thy countenance. May we believe that glory may dwell in the commonest task. For the sake of Jesus Christ our Lord we ask it. Amen.

J. H. JOWETT

1 October

On the bloodstained ground
Where the shadow falls
Of a cross and a crown of thorns
I kneel down, I kneel down
I lift up my eyes to a tear stained face
Who is this dying in my place
I kneel down, I kneel down

I come just as I am
This is my only plea
One hope in which I trust
This blood was shed for me

As you wash the stains of my guilty heart
Til I'm clean in every part
I kneel down, I kneel down
Wash away my shame, my pain, my pride
Every sin that I once denied
I kneel down, I kneel down

This is where I'll always come
This is where I'll always run
To worship you
This is where I'll always come
This is where I'll always run
To worship you, Jesus

GRAHAM KENDRICK

2 October

O Lord our Heavenly Father, Almighty and everlasting God, who hast safely brought us to the beginning of this day, defend us in the same with thy mighty power, and grant that this day we fall into no sin, neither run into any kind of danger; but that all our doings may be ordered by thy governance, to do always that is righteous in thy sight; through Jesus Christ our Lord. Amen.

GELASIAN SACRAMENTARY

Holy Spirit of God,
Hide the preacher, that he may be forgotten.
Reveal the Saviour,
that his voice may be heard,
His will obeyed,
and His Name honoured
to the glory of God the Father. Amen.

KEITH WESTON
(*a prayer given before preaching*)

3 October

The choir of stars fill us with admiration for you,
as they declare that it is you that number them and name
them.
The animals too, declare that you put life into them;
the trees show that you make them grow.
You have created all things,
and they display the greatness of your power.
Everyone ought to send up a hymn from their
souls to you,
through Christ,
for you are kind in your benefits,
and full of compassion.
You alone are almighty.
There is no God besides you,
there is none holy besides you,
you are the Lord,
the God of knowledge,
the God of the saints,
holy above all holy beings.
You are glorious,
and highly exalted,
invisible by nature,
and unsearchable in your judgements.

APOSTOLIC CONSTITUTIONS

4 October

O God our Father, give to us, Lord, what Thou seest fit; only fit us for what Thou givest, and let it bring to our souls health and peace, with some good to our neighbour and the world, for Thy goodness' sake, O Lord.

Make me to Thyself a temple of holy things, and abiding with me, O Lord, at the last, be ever gracious unto Thy servant.

Let me do some work which may be accepted in Thy mercy, though unworthy in Thy pure sight.

Bless my work to good, to the fullness of which it is capable, and let me thank Thee for it with joy in the end.

Into Thy hands we commend our spirit, soul, and body, of which Thou art Creator, Saviour, Restorer, a God of truth.

Lord, to Thee I commit my going out and my coming in this day. Amen.

ROWLAND WILLIAMS

5 October

Our Father, we are very weak. Worst of all we are very wicked if left to ourselves, and we soon fall a prey to the enemy. Therefore help us. We confess that sometimes in prayer when we are nearest to Thee at that very time some evil thought comes in, some wicked desire. Oh! what poor simpletons we are. Lord help us. We feel as if we would now come closer to Thee still, and hide under the shadows of Thy wings. We wish to be lost in God. We pray that Thou mayest live in us, and not we live, but Christ live in us and show Himself in us and through us.

Lord sanctify us; use every power of our nature for obedience to God.

C. H. SPURGEON

6 October

Father God,
I keep falling and failing, please pick me up and forgive me and heal me.

I've got so many irons in the fire, I've put the fire out. Help me to take some irons out of the fire, and by your Holy Spirit stoke up the flame of fire in me.

Lord, if I don't live by priorities, I'm going to live by pressures. Show me your priorities for my life. Give me the wisdom to discern your will.

Jesus, not only do I desire to be like you in character but to be like you in conduct. May your Holy Spirit produce love, joy, peace, patience, kindness, goodness, faithfulness, gentleness and self-control in me.

Help me to reflect you in thought, word and deed.

In Jesus' name.

Amen.

J. JOHN

7 October

O Lord, take us into Thy care and keeping; lest our cruel enemy gain the advantage over us. We fight under Thy banner, that our enemy may know that our confidence is in Thy aid, in Thy strength and wisdom.

Where Thou art, O Lord, is the land of liberty, and of everlasting blessedness. Give quietness to our minds, and grant that we may have some taste of the everlasting joys of Thy heavenly kingdom; whereby those worldly things which we so earnestly seek and so eagerly embrace, shall seem loathsome and defiled. So shall we refuse them as bitter and worthless things, and fervently desire the blessedness of Thy heavenly kingdom, where there are pleasures for evermore. And unto Thee, Lord Jesus, be glory for ever and ever. Amen.

THOMAS CRANMER

8 October

Hosanna in the highest!
Remember me, O Lord,
with the favour that Thou bearest unto Thy people.
O visit me with Thy salvation;
that I may see the felicity of Thy chosen,
and rejoice in the gladness of Thy people,
and give thanks with Thine inheritance.
There is glory which shall be revealed;
for when the Judge cometh
some shall see Thy face cheerful,
and shall be placed on the right,
and shall hear those most welcome words,
'Come, ye blessed.'
They shall be caught up in clouds
to meet the Lord;
they shall enter into gladness,
they shall enjoy the sight of Him,
they shall be ever with Him.

LANCELOT ANDREWES

9 October

Through death immortality has come to all, and through the incarnation of the Word God's universal providence has been made known. God the Word revealed himself through a body that we might receive an idea of the unseen Father; and he endured humiliation at men's hands that we might inherit incorruption. In himself he was in no way injured, for he is impassible and incorruptible, the very Word and God; but he endured these things for the sake of suffering men, and through his own impassibility he preserved and saved them. In short, the victories achieved by the Saviour through his incarnation are so great and so many that, if one wished to describe them, it would be like gazing across the open sea and trying to count the waves.

ST ATHANASIUS

10 October

It is not that I feel less weak, but Thou
Wilt be my strength; it is not that I see
Less sin; but more of pardoning love with Thee,
And all-sufficient grace. Enough! And now
All fluttering thought is stilled; I only rest,
And feel that Thou art near, and know that I am blest.

FRANCES RIDLEY HAVERGAL

We beseech Thee, Almighty God, to behold our prayers, and to pour out upon us Thy loving tenderness; that we who are afflicted by reason of our sins, may be refreshed by the coming of our Saviour; through the same Jesus Christ our Lord. Amen.

GELASIAN SACRAMENTARY

11 October

Preserve us, O most holy Lord God, from the cares of this life; that our feet be not entangled by them: and deliver us from spiritual hindrances and temptations, that we be not wearied and cast down; let not the world and the things of the world deceive us: keep us from the power and malice of the devil. Rather than all this world's allurements, give us the blessed unction of Thy Holy Spirit; and drive from our hearts the love of worldly things, by pouring into them the love of Thy holy name.

Confirm us in Thy ways, O Lord, by the grace of Thy Holy Spirit. Strengthen us with might so that no trouble or temptation may draw us away from Thee.

THOMAS À KEMPIS

12 October

O Heavenly Father, have mercy upon me; and pardon whatever you have seen amiss in me today, whether of thought or word or deed. Keep a clean and pure heart within me, O God, and renew a right spirit within me, that I may walk before You in holiness and righteousness all the days of my life. Through Jesus Christ my Lord.

MAURICE ROWLANDSON

Lord, You alone know how much patience I need. Open my eyes when I have difficult times and trials, to help me see them from Your side and to realise that they are meant to teach me patience.

CORRIE TEN BOOM

13 October

Grant unto us, Almighty God, in all time of distress, the comfort of the forgiveness of our sins. In time of darkness give us blessed hope, in time of sickness of body give us quiet courage; and when the heart is bowed down, and the soul is very heavy, and life is a burden, and pleasure a weariness, and the sun is too bright, then may that Spirit, the Spirit of the Comforter, come upon us, and after our darkness may there be the clear shining of the heavenly light; that so, being uplifted again by Thy mercy, we may pass on through this our mortal life with quiet courage, patient hope, and unshaken trust, hoping through Thy loving-kindness and tender mercy to be delivered from death into the large life of the eternal years. Hear us in Thy mercy, through Jesus Christ our Lord. Amen.

GEORGE DAWSON

14 October

Dear Lord, may I take Thee with me today 'in my heart', do nothing that would grieve Thee, say nothing that I should be ashamed to say in Thy physical presence, think nothing that is unworthy, and go nowhere, where I should be ashamed to be found by Thee. Let the thought of Thy real presence with me dominate my life today. Amen.

LESLIE WEATHERHEAD

O Saviour, since Thou, the Lord of heaven and earth, didst humble Thyself, grant unto us true humility, and make us like Thyself. And then, of Thine infinite goodness, raise us to Thine everlasting glory, who livest and reignest with the Father, and the Holy Ghost, for ever and ever. Amen.

THOMAS CRANMER

15 October

O Father, this day may bring some hard task to our life, or some hard trial to our love. We may grow weary, or sad, or hopeless in our lot. But, Father, our whole life until now has been one great proof of Thy care. Bread has come for our body, thoughts to our mind, love to our heart, and all from Thee. May this day be full of a power that shall bring us near to Thee, and make us more like Thee; and, O God, may we so trust Thee this day that, when the day is done, our trust shall be firmer than ever. Then, when our last day comes, and our work is done, may we trust Thee in death and forever, in the spirit of Jesus Christ our Lord. Amen.

ROBERT COLLYER

16 October

O Lord,
When did I last stop
Alone, in the dark,
To look at the heavens,
To see them as the work of your hands?
That's one of the many things in this busy life
That we might do more often.

But I have looked:
Through light years and incalculable distances
Past the familiar names of unimaginable words –
Pulsars and Red Dwarfs and Black Holes –
Whose very meanings I do not understand.

My fingers are the work of your fingers too.
The busy mechanism, the cells and tissue,
Nerves and muscles,
Whorled and wrinkled skin,
The sense, the cunning, and quick obedience:
You made us all, our world and all our worlds,
O Lord, my Lord.

O majestic Lord, you care for me,
In that I rest.

Amen.

TIMOTHY DUDLEY-SMITH

17 October

May the heavenly intercession of thy beloved Son so prevail on behalf of thy Church that, constrained by divine love, it may proclaim the Gospel to all the world until every nation becomes his inheritance and the uttermost parts of the earth are the possession of his Kingdom.

THOMAS TORRANCE

Lord Jesus Christ,

Long ago in the synagogue someone took the scroll of Holy Scripture and put it into your hands so that you might open it, read it, and use it to point to yourself: please take the Bibles we now hold and reveal yourself to us. As with those who walked to Emmaus open to us the Scriptures, fill our minds with their truth, cause our hearts to burn within us, and send our feet out in new directions.

We ask it for your Name's sake.

ALEC MOTYER

18 October

Almighty and eternal God, there is no number of Thy days or of Thy mercies: Thou hast sent us into this world to serve Thee, and to live according to Thy laws. O dear Lord, look upon us in mercy and pity: let Thy Holy Spirit lead us through this world with safety and peace, comforts and joy in the Holy Ghost; that when we have served Thee in our generation, we may be gathered unto our fathers, having the testimony of a holy conscience, in the confidence of a certain faith, and the comforts of a holy hope, that neither death nor life, nor angels nor principalities, nor powers, nor things present, nor things to come, nor height, nor depth, nor any other creature, may be able to separate us from the love of God, which is in Jesus Christ our Lord. Amen.

JEREMY TAYLOR

19 October

Arise, O Spirit of Life, that through Thee we may begin to live; descend upon us and transform us into such human beings as the heart of God longs to see us, renewed into the image of Christ, and going on from glory to glory. O God, Thou Supreme Good, make Thyself known to us, and glorify Thyself in our inner being. Amen.

GERHARD TERSTEEGEN

Your eternal power quenches flame,
stops the mouths of lions,
raises up the sick,
and overrules the power of all things.

You are he who is in heaven,
he who is on earth,
he who is in the sea,
he who is in finite things,
for you are not confined by anything,
and of your majesty there is no boundary.

APOSTOLIC CONSTITUTIONS

20 October

O Lord Jesus Christ, Who for our sakes didst become poor, we pray Thee to protect them that are rich in this world, that they may be not high-minded, nor trust in uncertain riches, but in Thee, the living God, Who givest us richly all things to enjoy. Grant them grace so to use their wealth that they may do good, and be rich in good words, ready to distribute and willing to communicate; laying up in store for themselves a good foundation against the time to come, that they may lay hold on eternal life; through Jesus Christ our Lord. Amen.

SURSUM CORDA

21 October

Lord, as you look into my heart and see the hypocrisy, sin and lack of fruitfulness you must wonder if I really do love you because I am not as obviously born again as you mean me to be.

Lord, I acknowledge my deep, deep, need of you to wash, cleanse and renew. Thank you for your patience, power and forgiveness. May my life increasingly bear the marks of your healing and inspiring touch.

Lord, may my chief and only concern be for your glory. May the Holy Spirit live in me in complete fullness and authority producing the life of Jesus in me.

Lord, I ask that the peace, humility, grace and love of Jesus may shine through my mortal flesh. Amen.

GEORGE RUSSELL

22 October

O My God, Thou and Thou alone art all-wise and all-knowing! I believe that Thou knowest just what is best for me. I believe that Thou lovest me better than I love myself, that Thou art all-wise and all-powerful. I thank Thee, with all my heart, that Thou hast taken me out of my own keeping, and hast bidden me to put myself in Thy hands. I can ask nothing better than this, to be Thy care, not my own. O my Lord, through Thy grace, I will follow Thee whithersoever Thou goest, and will not lead the way. I will wait on Thee for Thy guidance, and, on obtaining it, I will act in simplicity and without fear. And I promise that I will not be impatient, if at any time I am kept by Thee in darkness and perplexity; nor will I complain or fret if I come into any misfortune or anxiety. Amen.

JOHN HENRY NEWMAN

23 October

O God, Who hast taught us to keep all Thy heavenly commandments by loving Thee and our neighbour: grant us the
spirit of peace and grace, that we may both be devoted to
Thee with our whole heart, and united to each other with a
pure will; through Jesus Christ our Lord. Amen.

BOOK OF CONGREGATIONAL PRAYER, 1920

Lord, help us, we implore Thee, to resolve that we will trust
Thee this day to shine into any gloom of the mind, to stand
by us in any trial of our love, and to give us rest in Thy
good time as we need.

ROBERT COLLYER

24 October

This is a direct translation of a deaf person's prayer in British sign language and the structure is different from spoken English.

O Lord you great wonderful powerful God
I praise worship adore you always
I know you love always same for ever me everybody
No matter deaf hearing anything
I thank Jesus died my sins took all away make free
I know you can't hear me but can see my signing you
Because you God can hear and see all people pray you
I happy always because you can answer signing prayers
I know you can sign me Holy Spirit inside me
I really happy I can hear you Spirit me
Lord draw more Deaf you Jesus loves them always
Thank you Lord God ever ever Jesus Name
Amen

DAVID BUXTON

25 October

Gracious and glorious Lord, the eyes of all wait upon Thee; Thou art the hope of all the ends of the earth. In Thee we live and move and have our being; Thou givest us life and breath, and all things. Thy mercies are daily bestowed upon us; Thy goodness is new every morning.

Give us grace to acknowledge Thee in all our ways, and be Thou graciously pleased to establish our goings, and to direct our paths. Grant us Thy fatherly protection, and the heavenly guidance of Thy good Spirit, to choose our inheritance for us, and to dispose of us, and all that belongs to us, to the glory of Thy great Name.

AUGUSTUS TOPLADY

26 October

O Thou who art the Only Life; Thou by whom all things live; Thou biddest us to seek Thee; and art ready to be found. Thou biddest us to knock, and art ready to open. To depart from Thee is to fall into eternal death; to return to Thee is salvation; to abide in Thee is security and strength. To know Thee is life; to serve Thee is perfect freedom; to praise and adore Thee is the joy of Thy people. We worship Thee, we glorify Thee, we give thanks to Thee for Thy great glory, O holy Lord God Almighty.

ST AUGUSTINE

27 October

Heavenly Father, thank You for what You have done for me in the past. You have led me in my earlier life and will also lead on into the future. Deepen my confidence and trust in You. I know that all life advances. The years come and go, sometimes more quickly than I can believe. Help me to adjust to all change, knowing that the best is yet to be. In the name of Your Son, our great unchanging Christ. I pray.

O God, give me the insight and imagination I need to make each stage distinctive and beautiful. Help me adjust to all of life's changes and to beautify the hours, days and months as they come and go.

Father, if the fires of my life are tending to burn low, don't let them go out. As I go along I am gathering experiences. Help me turn all my experiences into expression and pass on to others what you have taught me.

SELWYN HUGHES

28 October

Almighty God, our heavenly Father, who hast promised to hear the prayers which are offered up in the name of Thy beloved Son, we beseech thee, for our Lord Jesus Christ's sake, that of Thy boundless mercy Thou wouldst pardon our sins, and wouldst so draw our thoughts unto thyself, that we may call upon Thee from our inmost heart, and desire such things as are according to Thy will.

Grant these petitions, O merciful Father, for Thy dear Son's sake, Jesus Christ, our Lord. Amen.

JOHN CALVIN

Grant, we beseech Thee, merciful Lord, to Thy faithful people pardon and peace, that they may be cleansed from all their sins, and serve Thee with a quiet mind. Through Jesus Christ our Lord. Amen.

BOOK OF COMMON PRAYER

29 October

O God of infinite love, Who didst give Thine only Son to suffer death upon the Cross for our redemption; We laud and magnify Thy glorious name; we praise Thee, we bless Thee, we worship Thee, we glorify Thee, we give thanks to Thee for Thy great glory; O Lord God, heavenly King, God the Father Almighty.

Keep us, good Lord, amid the temptations of life. Lead us not into temptation, but deliver us from the evil one. Be Thou our shield and defence. Guide, guard, and protect us. Help us to watch and pray that we enter not into temptation. And to Thee, O Lord: Father, Son, and Holy Ghost, be ascribed all might, majesty, dominion and glory, now and for ever more. Amen.

THOMAS HALL

30 October

O Lord, what shall this day bring forth! Fill the house with thy calm peace. Speak to me, O Lord, how hungry I am for Thee and Thy ways and word. Nothing to perceive but just Thyself. Lord, take the elaborate and the heroic and the impulsive and give me to quietly wait on Thee.

'Like rain upon the mown grass'; 'as the dew unto Israel' – O Lord, these phrases come to my mind this morning with a sweet insistence. Be as rain and as dew unto us to-day, refreshing, remoulding and blessing us. Unto Thee do I come in great and glad expectancy.

OSWALD CHAMBERS

31 October

Blessed Jesus, who didst with thine own heart's blood redeem each one of Thy members, wilt Thou not with more of Thine own Spirit baptise thy people, that this people, perishing for lack of knowledge, may also be fed with living manna, and have the light of life!

JAMES HUDSON TAYLOR

We give thee hearty thanks, O God, for the rest of the past night and for the gift of a new day with its opportunities of pleasing thee. Grant that we so pass its hours in the perfect freedom of thy service, that at eventide we may again give thanks unto thee; through Jesus Christ our Lord. Amen.

DAYBREAK OFFICE
OF THE EASTERN CHURCH

1 November

Holy Spirit, move among the nations as you moved over the face of the waters in the beginning, bring light and life to those who sit in darkness and in the shadow of death.

O God, the days are numbered and the time is short. Send forth into your harvest field the labourers for the Gospel your world so needs, that the earth may be filled with the glory of God as the waters cover the sea. Then come, Lord Jesus: thy kingdom come, thy will be done on earth as it is in heaven, when every knee shall bow and every tongue confess that Jesus Christ is Lord, to the glory of your Name. Amen.

KEITH WESTON

2 November

O God, early in the morning do I cry unto Thee.
Help me to pray, and to think only of Thee.
I cannot pray alone.
In me there is darkness,
But with Thee there is light.

I am lonely
    but Thou leavest me not.
I am feeble in heart,
    but Thou leavest me not.
I am restless,
    but with Thee there is peace.
In me there is bitterness,
    but with Thee there is patience.
Thy ways are past understanding,
    but Thou knowest the way for me.

DIETRICH BONHOEFFER

Fill our hearts with deep compassion for those who suffer,
and hasten the coming of Thy kingdom of justice and
truth; for the sake of Jesus Christ our Lord. Amen.

EUGÈNE BERSIER

3 November

O Thou Who art the strength of all souls, guide us through the darkness of this world, guard us from its perils, hold up and strengthen us when we grow weary and lead us by Thy chosen paths, through time and through death, to our eternal home in Thy heavenly kingdom: through Jesus Christ our Lord. Amen.

BOOK OF CONGREGATIONAL PRAYER, 1920

O Lord, keep us from sin this day. Subdue our iniquities, and assist us with Thy grace. Sanctify to us all our employments, our comforts, and our troubles; every condition of life, and every event that shall befall us.

AUGUSTUS TOPLADY

4 November

Gracious and Holy Father,
Give us wisdom to perceive You,
intelligence to understand You,
diligence to seek You,
patience to wait for You,
eyes to behold You,
hearts to meditate upon You,
and a life to proclaim You,
through the power of the Holy Spirit of Jesus Christ, our
Lord.

ST BENEDICT

O God our Saviour, return and have compassion upon us,
for from Thee are all good things, and from Thee is all our
health. Hear us, O heavenly Father, for the sake of Thine
only Son, Jesus Christ, our Lord, who liveth and reigneth
with Thee and the Holy Ghost, now and for ever. Amen.

ST AUGUSTINE

5 November

May our cares never become anxieties. May our carefulness never reach anxiety, dividing and distracting the mind. Let none of Thy precious gifts be snares to us. May they all help us to serve and honour Thee.

There are some things in which we cannot make progress; but we ask that we may make progress in acquaintance with the unsearchable riches of Christ.

SAMUEL MARTIN

Grant to us, Lord, the spirit to think and do always such things as be right, that we, who cannot do anything that is good without thee, may by thee be enabled to live according to thy will; through Jesus Christ our Lord. Amen.

BOOK OF COMMON PRAYER

6 November

O Lord Jesus, who, in the heaviness of Thy soul, didst fall down in prayer unto Thy heavenly Father, grant us Thy grace, and the aid of Thy Holy Spirit, that we likewise, in all heaviness of mind, and in every time of trouble, may fly, by instant and earnest prayer, to the aid and comfort of our heavenly Father. Hear us, O Lord Jesus, for Thy name's sake. Amen.

THOMAS CRANMER

7 November

Forgive me when I ask You to fashion me according to Your will but then express surprise at the testings You send or permit in my life. Forgive me for failing to submit to Your chastening and even allowing bitterness into my heart.

I praise You for disciplining me always in love, only for my good, to share in Your holiness. I praise You that in all that happens You work it together for good, whether I see it in this life or must wait till the next.

When greater trials come, help me to remember this prayer, joyfully submitting to Your fatherly control. In the name of Christ who Himself learned obedience through suffering, living to praise You. Amen.

DEREK PRIME

8 November

Help me not merely to enjoy reading beautiful words and call it praying. Make me utterly sincere, not using false exaggeration to show myself in a more favourable light at another's cost.

Help me to watch for that negativism that spreads depression and imprisons me in weakness. Help me today to rejoice in goodness, beauty and truth, forget myself and gratefully look to Thee and serve others. Help me to smile, to speak lovingly and cheerfully; trusting when I feel beaten and acting serenely when all is tempest within.

Master, casting out devils in Galilee was small compared with Thy task in me when anger and self-pity are roused! Come, bring Thy peace. Amen.

LESLIE WEATHERHEAD

9 November

Lord, who in the beginning did make the world, have regard to the prayer of Thy unworthy servant. Open mine eyes that I may see how near Thou art to me. It is a mystery, deep and wide, that Thou shouldest deign to enter my heart, and be my guest. Be also my Host; let me live in Thee, and do Thou live in me more and more. Let no folly or sin of mine make Thy presence impossible; save me from banishing Thee from my heart. Make Thy presence, Lord, an increasing power in my life; let it become the supreme fact and factor of my daily existence. Let all my decisions – small and great – be made in Thy light.

WALTER JAMES

10 November

Father God, I stand amazed and humbled in your presence when I think that you the eternal God, the Creator, the Almighty, should love me, indeed all mankind, so much that you sent Jesus into this world to deal with our sin problem. I thank and praise you for Jesus and His uniqueness,

(i)   in His birth – born of a virgin
(ii) in His life – always doing your will
(iii) in His death – he alone could pay the price for sin.

But I praise you, Father, that I do not worship a dead Saviour but rather one who conquered death, ascended to heaven and is now seated in the place of power at your right hand.

Father, because Jesus gave His life for me at Calvary, enable me to give my all for Him and live, articulate and defend my Faith so that others may discover the Saviour for themselves.

This I ask in Jesus' name and for His glory. Amen.

DAVID McNEE

11 November

When we awake, we are still with thee, O God most merciful, and thy hand is over us for good. Be Thou the Desire of our hearts, and the Ruler of our thoughts. O heavenly Father, we need Thy love, and Thy calm breath shed abroad in our souls, to be a fountain of strength; we know not, without Thee, what may befall us this day, either of peril, or of temptation, or of sorrow. But thou canst put a guard about our path, and canst fence all our senses from temptation, by sobering them with Thy holy fear. Give us, then, we pray Thee, a right sense of duty, and guard us against sin and death. Lead us not into temptation; or, when we are tempted, deliver us by humble watchfulness from all power of evil, through Jesus Christ our Lord and Saviour. Amen.

ROWLAND WILLIAMS

12 November

Dear Lord, make me wholly Thine. Penetrate me wholly with Thyself, that Thou mayest be all in all in me; be Thou the Soul of my soul. Lord, I am weary of myself, weary of being so unlike Thee, of being so far away from Thee. Abide with me, then – abide in me. Let no sorrow keep me away from Thee; let no loneliness or desolation of soul affright me. Let me not think of Thee as one afar off; let me not think of Thee as a severe judge, since Thou Thyself comest unto me, and fallest on the neck of Thy poor prodigal, and givest me the kiss of peace. Thou wilt not let those go empty away who come to Thee from far. Lord, I am come to Thee from far, the far-off land of my miseries and my sins. But Thou hast brought me near. Amen.

E. B. PUSEY

13 November

May it please Thee to forget all our sins past, and of Thy infinite mercy freely to pardon them, according as Thou hast promised to all them that call upon Thee with a true heart. Grant us these our petitions, O Father of mercy, for our Lord and Saviour, Jesus Christ's sake. Amen.

LITURGY OF GENEVA

And now, O God, our hope is in Thee. Be with us in all the duties that await us. Make Thy grace sufficient for us. And grant that all the words of our mouths, and all the meditations of our hearts, may be acceptable in thy sight, through Jesus Christ, our Lord and only Saviour. Amen.

PRAYERS FOR SOCIAL AND FAMILY WORSHIP
(by the Church of Scotland)

14 November

Our Heavenly Father,
Liberate us today from slavery to circumstances and from
dependency upon external conditions of advantage.

Strengthen our faith in the midst of trials as the mighty
oak strengthens its roots during many storms.

Let our hearts revel with the joy that through the trials
Thou dost perfect our maturity so that we lack nothing.

In Thy perfecting work we learn the secret of wisdom
without lack and faith without doubt. Further, Thy promise
guarantees us a crown of life without tarnish.

No longer in bondage to serving self, may we live in the
liberating freedom of serving as the 'slaves of Christ' in
Whose Name we make our prayer with thanksgiving.
Amen.

JOHN EDMUND HAGGAI

15 November

For the Holy Spirit who dwells in our hearts, strengthening us in weakness, guiding us in perplexity, convicting us of sin, comforting us in sorrow, changing us into the likeness of Christ:
With grateful hearts, We thank Thee, O God. Amen.

SCRIPTURE UNION PRAYERS FOR SCHOOLS, YOUTH GROUPS, CHURCH SERVICES AND PERSONAL USE

16 November

Lord, unto Thee do I come that I might find grace to worship Thee aright. Lift up the light of Thy countenance upon us and give us peace. Touch me now with that thrilling touch that makes all the difference between full life and mere existence.

'The Lord God Omnipotent reigneth!' Lord, make this day a great and glorious one, filled with grace and glory and preciousness. Lead us, O Lord, in deep and great and hearty intercession throughout this day.

OSWALD CHAMBERS

17 November

O Lord God! the Fountain of all Fullness, we, who are nothing but emptiness, come unto Thee for all supplies, nor shall we come in vain, since we come commanded by Thy Word, encouraged by Thy promise, and preceded by Christ Jesus, our great High Priest, we know that whatsoever we shall ask in prayer, believing, we shall receive. Only do Thou help us now to ask right things, and may the utterances of our mouth be acceptable in Thy sight, O God our Strength and our Redeemer.

We would adore Thy blessed and ever-to-be-beloved Name. Oh! that men for whom the Saviour shed His blood, loved Thee with all their hearts.

The faithful, chosen, called and separated, join in the everlasting song. All Thy redeemed praise Thee, O God! As the God of our election we extol Thee for Thine everlasting and immutable love.

C. H. SPURGEON

18 November

Lord God, we cry to you, fill us with your Holy Spirit, baptise us in your love and send us in your strength to minister Christ to those we meet. Give us great confidence in the message of the gospel, open doors of opportunity for us and enable us with courage and sensitivity to speak of Jesus.

Heavenly Father, we long that the prayer of Jesus may be answered in our lives; 'As the Father has sent me, I am sending you.' Send us afresh with his sense of commission and his heart of compassion. Use us, even today, to bring someone to you. Amen.

VICTOR JACK

19 November

O Lord, who hast given us Thy sun to gladden us with light and to ripen the fruits of the earth for our support, and to set when his work is done, that he may rise again tomorrow; give Thy blessing to us Thy servants, that the lesson of the works of Thy hand may be learnt by us Thy living works, and that we may run our course like the sun which is now gone from us.

Let us rise early and go late to rest, being every busy and zealous in doing Thy will. Let our light shine before men, that they may glorify Thee, our Heavenly Father. Let us do good all our days, and be useful to and comfort others. And let us finish our course in faith, that we too may rise again to a course which shall never end.

THOMAS ARNOLD

20 November

We come unto our father's God. Their Rock is our Foundation. O Thou God of our fathers be, we beseech Thee, the Guide of their succeeding race ... In this hour of restlessness and turmoil lead us into the secret place. Lift us above the clash of the hour. The air is charged with calamity and our hearts are strangely moved. Make Thy way manifest, even though overtures of peace have broken down. In the hour of our extremity we turn to Thee ... If it be decreed in the awful and perfect counsel of Thy holy will, that we can be purged and redeemed only through suffering, grant to all of us who bear Thy holy Name a quietness and resignation of Spirit such as shall make us strong in the hour of our chastisement!

G. CAMPBELL MORGAN

21 November

O Lord God, we bless thee, for Jesus Christ and His great salvation, for the covenant of grace made with us in Him, and for all the exceeding great and precious promises and privileges of that covenant; for the throne of grace to which we may come in His name with humble boldness, and for the blessed hope of eternal life through Him. We confess that we have sinned and done foolishly. O Lord, Thou knowest our foolishness, and our sins are not hidden from Thee. Who can understand his errors; O cleanse Thou us from our secret faults.

We pray Thee to give us repentance for our sins and make us sensible of the evil of them, and let the blood of Christ cleanse us from them.

MATTHEW HENRY

22 November

Lord, the creatures of Thy hand, Thy children, come before Thee with their wishes and regrets: Children we are, children we shall be, till our mother the earth hath fed upon our bones. Accept us, correct us, guide us, Thy guilty innocents. Dry our vain tears, wipe out our vain resentments, help our yet vainer efforts. Be patient still; suffer us yet awhile longer – with our broken purposes of good, with our idle endeavours against evil, suffer us awhile longer to endure, and (if it may be) help us to do better. We thank Thee and praise Thee.

ROBERT LOUIS STEVENSON

23 November

Glory to our ascended Lord that He is with us always.
Glory to the Word of God, going forth with His armies
        conquering and to conquer.
Glory to Him Who has led captivity captive and given
        gifts for the perfecting of His saints.
Glory to Him Who has gone before to prepare a place in
        His Father's home for us.
Glory to the Author and Finisher of our Faith; that God
        in all things may be glorified through Jesus
        Christ,
To Whom be all worship and praise, dominion and
        glory; now and for ever and ever. Amen.

SURSUM CORDA

24 November

O Light eternal, transcending all created suns, cause Thy bright beams to shine into our hearts. Purify, warm, enlighten, and quicken our souls with all their powers: so that they may find their rest, their joy, in Thee.

The days of this present life are short and evil, full of troubles and sorrows: when wilt Thou bring the reign of Satan to an end: and grant to us to walk at liberty, without trials or temptations, seeing Thy face, and wearing Thy likeness? Until then, preserve us, O Thou eternal Truth; come unto us, O heavenly Love; draw our affections away from earthly things, and fix them upon Thyself. Blessed are they, O Lord, whom Thou choosest, and whom Thou causest to approach unto Thee.

THOMAS À KEMPIS

25 November

Grant, O heavenly Father, that we so faithfully believe in Thee, and so fervently love one another, always living in Thy fear, and in the obedience of Thy holy law and blessed will, that we, being fruitful in all good works, may lead our life according to Thy good pleasure in this world and, after this frail and short life, obtain the true and immortal life, where thou livest and reignest, world without end. Amen.

THOMAS BECON

O merciful Lord, of Thy bountiful goodness, receive us evermore into Thy protection, maintaining and increasing from day to day Thy grace and goodness towards us, until Thou hast brought us unto the full and perfect unity of Thy Son, Jesus Christ our Lord, who is the true light of our souls.

LITURGY OF GENEVA

26 November

Lord Jesus Christ, grant me Your special grace to speak Your Truth in love and to challenge every way that would exclude Love from Truth or Truth from Love. You who are both Truth and Love, enter my poor heart and mind afresh to bring forth this miracle of Truthful Love and Loving Truth for which I pray in Your most worthy Name. Amen.

MICHAEL CASSIDY

Come, Holy Spirit, and daily increase in us thy manifold gifts of grace; the spirit of wisdom and understanding; the spirit of counsel and ghostly strength; the spirit of knowledge and true godliness, and fill us with the spirit of thy holy fear, now and for ever. Amen.

GELASIAN SACRAMENTARY

27 November

Father, I want to be like you. I want my heart to be as big as yours.

As far as revival is concerned, I ask you to find those who will be guileless and entrust them with the wonderful treasures of your power and your presence. Please don't hide from us because our hearts are divided. Make us one big family rejoicing in your love.

Lord, I hunger for your word, but I don't believe that knowing you is only about memorising scripture or learning about how you've moved in the past. Knowing all that is valuable only if I can trust you like a little child.

I'm so glad, Father, that loving you with a childlike spirit is all that is necessary to please you, and knowing that makes me love you more.

JOHN ARNOTT

Lord, live so completely within me that all my life will be the natural outpouring of the divine power – the consequence of an indwelling Spirit of purity and truth.

WALTER JAMES

28 November

Loving heavenly Father, hallowed be thy name, thou art from everlasting to everlasting, the Father of my Saviour the Lord Jesus Christ and one with the Holy Spirit in the blessed Trinity. I come boldly but reverently into your holy presence in the name of Jesus. I come to you washed in the blood of the Lamb and knowing that I am holy and blameless in your sight, O God, by your altogether lovely Lord Jesus. I love you with all my heart, soul and mind. I am unworthy of your love, mercy and long-suffering. You have been generous to me and my family. Grant, I beseech, every gift of the Holy Spirit according to your sovereign will that I may lift up the name of Jesus for his glory alone. I confess I have sinned in word, thought and deed, that I have been unfaithful in the face of your faithfulness to me. Wash me in the blood of the Lamb for I am truly sorry for my sins. Renew in me the joy of my salvation. Grant me wisdom according to your promise, integrity and compassion that I may be fitted to serve you in the fulfilment of the Great Commission until Jesus comes to calls me home. All this I pray in the name of Jesus. Amen.

GRAHAM F. LACEY

29 November

O Lord, enable me to live the life of saints and angels. Take me out of the irritability, the sensitiveness, in which my soul lies, and fill it with Thy fullness.

Breathe on me with that Breath which infuses energy and kindles fervour. In asking for fervour, I ask for all that I can need, and all that Thou canst give. In asking for fervour, I am asking for faith, hope, and charity, in their most heavenly exercise; I am asking for perception of duty, I am asking for sanctity, peace, and joy, all at once. Nothing would be a trouble to me, nothing a difficulty, had I but a fervour of soul. Lord, in asking for fervour, I am asking for Thyself, for nothing short of Thee, O my God. Enter my heart, and fill it with fervour by filling it with Thee. Amen.

JOHN HENRY NEWMAN

30 November

Dear Heavenly Father, while I am on this journey through life, I pray that I may always listen for your voice, whether it is for praise or discipline. Please, *please* may I always know your presence, especially if I am to journey through life's valleys. When I am weak fill me with your strength, and help me to love like you love, even when it hurts. May nothing matter to me more than becoming the person you want me to be. Amen.

DIANNE PARSONS

1 December

Father, thank you for your reliability; for the energy of your Holy Spirit that causes the sun to rise. Thank you for the potential of this new day. Thank you that you have called and chosen me to work for you today and the power that causes the sun to rise is the same power that is at work by your Holy Spirit in my life. Let me not shrink back from anything today, but complete the work you have already ordained for me to do ... following the course you have set, not veering to the right or the left. May my heart beat in time with yours. May I see through your eyes. May I hear with understanding. Give me the determination and single-mindedness to keep sight of the vision and finish the job.

JULIA FISHER

2 December

Have pity upon us, O Lord, and look down upon us from the throne of Thy majesty; scatter the darkness of our souls, and enlighten us with the beams of Thy Holy Spirit.

Give us wisdom to discern between good and evil. Above all, we entreat of Thee full and free remission of all our sins; for Thou, O Lord Jesus, hast died to purchase it.

Lord, we pray Thee to bestow upon us everlasting life, not for our merits, but for Thy great mercy: upon which we cast ourselves as the only refuge and hope of sinners. Lord Jesus, hear us; heavenly Father, be merciful unto us; Holy Spirit, comfort us; and to Thy name, O blessed and holy Trinity, shall be praise and glory for ever and ever. Amen.

ST AUGUSTINE

3 December

You know me, Lord, my down-sitting and my uprising and you are acquainted with all my ways – the good, the bad and the indifferent, the right, the wrong, the Holy, the sinful, the ones that make you happy and the ones that make you sad. Lord, I read your Word and it says: 'I have seen his ways, BUT I will heal him.' You do know my ways and how far they fall short of your holiness, but nevertheless in grace and mercy you will heal me. Thank you, Lord. To be sure I can rest in nothing but the 'Buts' of God and the 'But God ...' words of a Heavenly Father full of grace and mercy for undeserving sinners such as I.

Thank you, Lord, Yes, thank you. Amen and Amen.

MICHAEL CASSIDY

4 December

O Lord Jesus, great is Thy goodness to them that seek Thee. Thou redeemest the captives; Thou art the Saviour of the lost, the strength of the weary, the freedom of the oppressed, the consolation of them that are cast down, the crown of the conquering, the reward and joy of Thy saints. O mighty God, may all things that are in heaven above and in the earth beneath bless Thee, for Thou art great, and great is Thy name. When Thou shalt come in Thy power and glory, raise us up, we beseech Thee, among Thy chosen, that in our flesh we may see Thy brightness, and be filled with the joy of Thy countenance.

ANSELM

5 December

Almighty God, I read that at the beginning it was dark. But suddenly you said, 'Let there be light.' And there was light. The world had never known the sun or the moon. It was as dark as it ever has been. But you decided it was time for light. No warning, no argument, no battle against the host of darkness. Just a decision.

At times for me the darkness is suffocation – it threatens to swamp me, sap me of hope, wear me down with its heaviness. But in heaven you watch. And when you decide the time is right the piercing light can come – in a moment. Lord, lighten my darkness.

ROB PARSONS

6 December

Forgive me, Lord, that my prayers are often nearly all asking, with too little praising. Yet I thank You that even this praises You because I trust only in Your faithfulness and steadfast love. Help me to fix my eyes upon You and make Your glory the starting-point of prayer, that my expectancy may know no limits.

Teach me when to be silent before You and when to speak, not missing hearing You through my eagerness to speak without listening. May I come in awe, because of Your greatness, and joy as I relax in Your presence, calling You 'Abba, Father'.

As I read Your Word reveal the truth about Yourself, that I may praise You more and more. Amen.

DEREK PRIME

7 December

Lord, nevertheless I am continually with You, although Your way is hidden from me. I know You uphold me with Your right hand. You lead me according to Your counsel, even when I see nothing but darkness. You make a path in the wilderness and cause me to reach the goal. Lord, I am ashamed that I was so defeated. Help me to realise Your sustaining presence is always there.

CORRIE TEN BOOM

8 December

There is no holiness, O Lord, if Thou withdraw Thine hand.

We are weak in ourselves, but strong in Thee; we are cold, till Thou warmest us with the warmth of life.

Blessed Jesus, grant us Thy grace; may it work with us, and in us, and continue with us to the end. Teach us to desire always that which is acceptable to Thee. Grant us to rest in Thee, and to enjoy in Thee that peace which the world cannot give.

THOMAS À KEMPIS

Look down upon thy servants with a patient eye, even as Thou sendest sun and rain: look down, quicken, enliven; recreate in us the soul of service, the spirit of peace; renew in us the sense of joy.

ROBERT LOUIS STEVENSON

9 December

Heavenly Father, how grateful we are for your steadfast love towards us when you could have justly abandoned us because of our rebellion and indifference towards you. We deserved to be excluded from your presence for ever and yet you came to visit us, clothed yourself with our humanity, experienced our earthly pain and even died, sacrificed yourself in order to save us. How privileged we are to be embraced with your love, to have received your forgiveness, to know your peace and to be called your children. Forgive us for our lack of moral courage to speak to friends and neighbours of your great love for them. We are ashamed that too often we are more concerned about our reputation than other people's salvation. Forgive us that we are so easily deceived by people's outward prosperity and apparent happiness that we no longer see them as lost, perishing and without hope.

VICTOR JACK

10 December

O God our Father, we thank thee for all thy loving care, and for giving us so many good things to enjoy; send us on our way now to do our duty through this day. Grant that we may always stand firm on the side of right, and spread thy Kingdom of happiness with thee and the Holy Spirit, one God, world without end. Amen.

PERCY DEARMER

O Christ, the Sun of Righteousness, Who didst manifest Thyself in our flesh, shine graciously into our hearts, that, walking as children of light, we may glorify Thee before men, and being always ready to obey Thy call, may, in our place, hold up the light of life to them that sit in darkness and the shadow of death. Hear us, O Lord, for Thy great mercies' sake, who livest and reignest with the Father and the Holy Ghost, now and for ever. Amen.

HENRY STOBART

11 December

O Holy Spirit, who art thyself the love with which the Father loves his Son and the Son loves the Father, let the love that thou art fill our hearts that we may share in the communion of the Father and the Son, and from that communion go forth to minister in the name and likeness of Jesus Christ our Lord.

THOMAS TORRANCE

Almighty God, who seest that we have no power of ourselves to help ourselves: keep us both outwardly in our bodies, and inwardly in our souls; that we may be defended from all adversities which may happen to the body, and from all evil thoughts which may assault and hurt the soul; through Jesus Christ our Lord. Amen.

GREGORIAN SACRAMENTARY

12 December

Our Father, I know well Thou canst never forsake those who seek Thee, nor disappoint those who trust Thee. Yet I know too, the more I pray for Thy protection, the more surely and fully I shall have it. And therefore now I cry out to Thee, first that Thou wouldest keep me from myself, and from following any will but Thine. Next, I beg of Thee, O my loving Lord – if it be not wrong so to pray – visit me not with those trying visitations which saints alone can bear! Pity my weakness, and lead me heavenwards in a safe and tranquil course. Still I leave all in Thy hands – only, if Thou shalt bring heavier trials on me, give me more grace, flood me with the fullness of Thy strength and consolation. Amen.

JOHN HENRY NEWMAN

13 December

God of all compassion, whose will is that none should perish in their sins but that all should come to repentance; have mercy upon the millions who have never heard of the saving grace of our Lord Jesus Christ, or who, having heard, have failed to respond to the Gospel.

Turn the tide of evil in our land and in lands across the world, that unbelief and ignorance of your Word and will may be transformed, and that men and women, loving you above all else, may learn to love each other. Purge from your world the hatred and inhumanity, the contempt and the violence.

KEITH WESTON

14 December

Lord, often, when I am longing to talk with my husband the phone rings or he's off to another church meeting. Please give me patience, and wisdom to carve out time together.

It's wearing being short of money and needing the whole PCC to agree before we replace the washing machine (which was probably salvaged from the Ark anyway). Please give me patience and wisdom about that too.

And when people criticise us and our ministry, I feel it so keenly and get lonely and depressed. Please send a friend I can share with, and thank You for all the kindness and love our congregation gives.

We're in this ministry together, as a couple, as a family. Every day we need Your help. Thank You for bringing us here and for Your promise to be with us, always. Amen.

CELIA BOWRING

15 December

O loving God, we thank Thee once more for the quiet rest
of the night that has gone by, for the new promise that has
come with this fresh morning, and for the hope of this day.
While we have slept, the world in which we live has swept
on in its awful space, great waters have been all about us,
and great storms above us: but Thou hast held them back
by Thy strong hand, and we have rested under the shadow
of Thy love. The bird sat on the spray out in the darkness,
the flower nestled in the grass, we lay down in our home,
and all slept in the arms of God. The bird will trust Thee
this day to give its morsel of meat, and the flower will trust
Thee for its fresh raiment; so may we trust Thee this day
for all the needs of the body, the soul, and the spirit. Amen.

ROBERT COLLYER

16 December

Lord, I'm a bit of a struggler.

In fact, I struggle far more than I ever dreamt I would. I struggle with life, and in my relationship with you, other people and even with myself.

Lord, I'm a bit of a doubter.

In fact, I doubt more than I ever dreamt I would. My motives are muddled, my vision confused – more than I like to acknowledge.

Lord, I'm more than a little frustrated.

In fact, I'm far more frustrated than I ever dreamt I'd be. I'm frustrated with myself for not listening. Worse yet, though I hardly dare admit it, I'm sometimes frustrated with you.

Still, I do love you and want to listen to your voice rather than mine. I want your will to be done.

So keep sorting me out. I know you love me and forgive my inconsistencies. That's why I'm here and trust you. And that's why I'm not going anywhere else.

STEVE CHALKE

17 December

Dearest Lord, may I see you today and every day in the person of your sick, and while nursing them, minister to you.

Even when you hide yourself behind the unattractive disguise of the irritable, the exacting, the unreasonable, may I still recognise you and gladly serve you.

O Jesus, bear with my faults, and look only at my intention, which is to love and serve you in the person of each of your sick. Lord, increase my faith, and bless my efforts and work, now and for evermore.

MOTHER TERESA

O Father Almighty; O Lord Jesus the Son of the Father; O Holy Spirit who proceedest from the Father and the Son, keep, we pray Thee, these creatures of Thy hand; who put their trust in Thee, and take refuge in Thy mercy.

ST AUGUSTINE

18 December

Father in the Highest, Who hast promised to dwell with them that are of a lowly spirit and fear Thy word; create now in us such lowly hearts, and give us a reverential awe of Thy commandments. O come, Thou Holy Spirit, and kindle our hearts with holy love; come, Thou Spirit of Strength, and arouse our souls to hunger and thirst after Thee, their true Guide, that they may be sustained by Thy all-powerful influence.

GERHARD TERSTEEGEN

O God, who hast prepared for them that love thee such good things as pass man's understanding, pour into our hearts such love towards thee, that we, loving thee above all things, may obtain thy promises, which exceed all that we can desire; through Jesus Christ our Lord. Amen.

GELASIAN SACRAMENTARY

19 December

Heavenly Father, whose Son Jesus Christ ministered full of grace and truth, help us so to receive him that we might increasingly reflect him. His truth has set us free and upon his grace we depend from start to finish of our Christian lives. Enable us to defend the truth, proclaim the truth, and live by the truth. Inspire us to do all in the spirit of gracious love so that Jesus may be seen in us.

We pray for your Church worldwide that it may never waver from the truth of the gospel. We pray for rebuke and restoration where it has gone astray and we ask that your people in these days may mirror the grace and truth of their Saviour and Lord Jesus Christ. Amen.

PHILIP HACKING

20 December

Lord, again we thank thee for thy word. We are prone to wander, detracting and subtracting from it, making things easy for ourselves, but we bless thee for this word, teaching and instructing us, warning and safeguarding us from the subtle assaults of the enemy who appears as an angel of light to twist and pervert even thy holy word.

Lord, we thank thee for the faith we have; may thou grant more clear assurance so we may give diligence to making our election sure. Thou has provided the way for this. Grant that your dear children may know as never before the Spirit bearing witness with them that they are the children of God, through Christ our Lord. Amen.

D. MARTYN LLOYD-JONES

21 December

Lord our God, thank you for all the love which our Lord Jesus Christ showed, while on earth, to those in need, the sick, the hungry, the outcasts. Help us to follow his example and, because of our love for you, and because he has commanded us, to love our neighbour as ourselves.

Lord, we know that if we do not show your love in our own lives, no one will believe in the God of love whom we preach; that if we care for the needs they feel, they may listen when we tell them of their greatest need of all, which they do not yet feel.

So Lord, as we feel your great love for us in sending your Son to die for us and his love in bearing our sin and being separated from you, may we feel that same love for our fellow men and women, all created by you in your image.

FRED CATHERWOOD

22 December

LONDON BRIDGES

God our Father,
we thank you for the privilege of living and working
    in this great city.
Help us by your Spirit to build bridges
    with love, courage, and hope
so that many will come to faith and life in you,
your love will be seen in action in our communities,
and we shall be renewed as your people for the new
    millennium.
We ask this through our Lord Jesus Christ,
who is himself the Bridge between you and all people
    through the cross,
and in whom we pass from darkness to light,
from death to resurrection.
Amen.

RICHARD CHARTRES

23 December

Dear Lord, we claim again the Joy we need to overcome our sins and sorrows and the thorns which infest our ground.

And do make Your blessings flow to wherever any curse or curses may be found.

In Your Name, O Lord, and by Your power, we break all curses directed at us or our loved ones.

We record them this day as broken,

And neutralised,

And banished.

And may we all now go out and prevail as far as the curse is found.

In Jesus' strong and all-prevailing Name we pray. Amen.

MICHAEL CASSIDY

24 December

A marvellous wonder has come to pass:
Nature is made new, and God becomes man.
That which he was, he has remained;
And that which he was not, he has taken on himself
While suffering neither confusion nor division.
How shall I tell of this great mystery?
He who is without flesh becomes incarnate;
The Word puts on a body;
The Invisible is seen;
He whom no hand can touch is handled;
And he who has no beginning now begins to be.
The Son of God becomes the Son of man:
Jesus Christ, the same yesterday, today and for ever.

THE ORTHODOX WAY
CHRISTMAS DAY VESPERS

25 December

O God, grant us to know that the one born of old in Bethlehem has also been born in our hearts; a living Christ within, never leaving us. O Lord, follow us to our homes, our work, wherever we go and in whatever we do. May we know thou wilt never forsake us, and witness the sweet intimations of thy nearness and grace.

Bless, O God, those who long to know thee better and the truth more truly. And now, may the grace of our Lord and Saviour Jesus Christ, the love of God and the fellowship of the Holy Spirit abide with us throughout the remainder of this our short and uncertain earthly pilgrimage and for ever more. Amen.

D. MARTYN LLOYD-JONES

26 December

Glory be to God in the highest, and on earth peace, good-will towards men. We praise Thee, we bless Thee, we glorify Thee, we give thanks unto Thee, for this greatest of Thy mercies, O Lord God, Heavenly King, God the Father Almighty. O Lord, the only begotten Son Jesus Christ, O Lord God, Lamb of God, Son of the Father, Who wast made man to take away the sins of the world, have mercy upon us by turning us from our iniquities. Thou Who wast manifested to destroy the works of the devil, have mercy upon us by enabling us to renounce and forsake them. Thou Who art the great Advocate with the Father, receive our prayer, we humbly beseech Thee. Amen.

THOMAS KEN

27 December

How excellent is Thy mercy, O God!
And the children of men shall put their trust
under the shadow of Thy wings.
The Lord bless us, and keep us,
and shew the light of His countenance upon us,
and be merciful unto us.
The Lord lift up His countenance upon us,
And give us peace!
I commend to Thee, O Lord,
my soul, and my body,
my mind, and my thoughts,
my prayers and my vows,
my senses, and my limbs,
my words, and my works,
my life, and my death.
Hear, O Lord, and have mercy upon me;
Lord, be Thou my helper.

LANCELOT ANDREWES

28 December

We thank Thee, Lord Jesus, that Thou, our High Priest before the throne of God, art ever living to make intercession for us. We thank Thee that Thou art touched with the feeling of our infirmity, and hast been in all points tempted like as we are yet without sin. Help us therefore to come boldly to Thy throne of Grace that we may obtain mercy, and find grace to help in time of need. Help us to watch and pray that we enter not into temptation. Strengthen our weakness by Thy divine strength, so shall we render to Thee, Lord Jesus, with the Father and the Holy Ghost, all honour and praise now and for evermore. Amen.

MATTHEW HENRY

29 December

God, are you there? The pain of not knowing where you are and if you even exist is more than I can bear.

I feel like heavy weights are pulling my heart from my chest. My heart is aching; the loneliness is so loud I cannot sleep.

My friends have walked away and now you have turned your back on me.

All my sins I have ever committed are coming before me. Must I now pay for my sins; did you not pay for them at Calvary? Am I going to die in this cell, do you hate me? Please forgive me.

It is hell without you. Please don't leave me alone. If you are there please do something to let me know you still love me.

I am scared in this place. I only live because I do not die. God let me die!

JIM BAKKER

30 December

Lord, help us to rise clean out of this world and its down-dragging tendencies, towards Thyself. We do not ask to be entranced by shining angels, but for Thy presence, Jesus, to be as if our eyes behold Thee and our fingers touched Thy nailprints. Thou hast ransomed Thy people with Thy heart's blood. Risen, ascended through the gates of pearl to Thy Father's throne we seem to see Thee, our ears almost catching the everlasting song rolling up at Thy feet. Over angelic squadrons Thou lookest and hearest our praises. Best Beloved, we have no one in Heaven but Thee; none upon earth we desire beside Thee. Father, Son and Holy Ghost accept us and in Jesus' name. Amen.

C. H. SPURGEON

31 December

May the fire of Christ consume all indifference to God
The light of Christ illumine our vision of God
The love of Christ enlarge our longing for God
The Spirit of Christ empower our service to God
And the Blessing of God Almighty,
The Father, the Son and the Holy Spirit
Be among us, and remain with us always.

JAMES JONES

Lord, when I die, the only things I want to leave behind are souls that are saved, lives that are happier, and situations that are better. Grant this, I pray, in Jesus' Name.

MICHAEL CASSIDY

Lord, grant that my last hour may be my best hour.

A.S.T. FISHER

Acknowledgments

While the authors and publisher have made every effort to contact the copyright holders of material used in this book, this has not always been successful. Full acknowledgment will gladly be made in future editions.

We gratefully acknowledge the following, extracts from which appear in this book:

Congregational Union of England and Wales, *Book of Congregational Worship* (Turnbull & Spears, 1920)

Dudley-Smith, Timothy, *Someone Who Beckons* (Inter-Varsity Press, 1978)

Kendrick, Graham, from *The Millennium Chorus*. Copyright © 1998 Ascent Music, PO Box 263, Croydon, Surrey, CR9 5AP, UK. International copyright secured. All rights reserved. Used by permission

Larcombe, Jennifer Rees, *Turning Point* (Hodder & Stoughton, 1994)

Lawrence, Brother, *The Practice of the Presence of God*, trans. E. M. Blaiklock (Hodder & Stoughton, 1981)

Prime, Derek, *Created to Praise* (Christian Focus Publications, 1981)

Redpath, Alan, *Victorians Praying* (Pickering & Inglis, 1957)

Robinson, Godfrey and Winward, Stephen, *Scripture Union Prayer Book* (Scripture Union, 1967)

Slater, William, *The Song of the Salvation Army* (The Salvation Army, 1953)

Scott, John, *Your Confirmation* (Hodder & Stoughton, 1991)

Ten Boom, Corrie, *This Day is the Lord's* (Hodder & Stoughton, 1980)

Tutu, Desmond, *An African Prayer Book*, Hodder & Stoughton, 1996)

Ware, Timothy, *The Orthodox Church* (Penguin Books, 1963)

Weatherhead, Leslie, *A Private House of Prayer* (Hodder & Stoughton, 1958)

Glossary

ACTS OF DEVOTION Devotional prayer book published in 1924. 184

ALCUIN OF YORK (c. 732–804) Master of York Cathedral School; Charlemagne's tutor and counsellor; established schools and libraries in France; poet; abbot of Tours. 209

ALFORD, HENRY (1810–71) Henry was born in Middlesex, and dedicated his life to God at the age of sixteen; Anglican minister in Wiltshire, Leicestershire and London – becoming Dean of Canterbury Cathedral in 1857; wrote hymns, including, 'Come ye thankful people, come'. 216, 247

AMESS, ROBERT (1944–) Robert was born in Bristol; he has been pastor of several churches in the UK, including Duke Street Baptist Church, Richmond; he is now the Chairman of the Evangelical Alliance. 129

ANDREWES, LANCELOT (1565–1626) Anglican Bishop of Ely and, later, Winchester; dean of the Royal Chapel to James I; now best known for his *Manual of Private Devotion and Meditation for the Visitation of the Sick;* involved in the Authorised Version translation team for parts of the Old Testament. 14, 39, 112, 164, 193, 237, 252, 257, 264, 282, 362

ANSELM (1033–1109) Anselm was born in Italy; he was awakened to a love of holy things and religious ideas by his mother when he was fifteen, and thereafter sought to conform to God's will; philosopher and theologian; developed the argument for the eternal self-existence of the divine nature known as the Ontological argument; reluctant Archbishop of Canterbury in 1093; known for his guileless simplicity, integrity, faithful zeal and patient

suffering for righteousness' sake. 15, 46, 109, 190, 253, 339

APOSTOLIC CONSTITUTIONS Multi-volume liturgical prayer book, written around 325 to 400. 45, 144, 180, 277, 293

AQUINAS, ST THOMAS (1224–74) Dominican theologian, born in Italy; was placed in his uncle's monastery at the age of five; Master of theology; stressed that Christian revelation and human knowledge are facets of a single truth and cannot be in conflict. 192

ARNDT, JOHANN (1555–1621) German Lutheran Minister who sought to restore the moral climate among German Protestants; wrote *One True Christianity*, a study of religious and practical influence on moral conduct (a book much valued by Wesley), and *The Garden of Paradise*, a book of prayers and spiritual exercises. 116

ARNOLD, DR THOMAS (1795–1842) Known as 'Poet Arnold' when young; chaplain, then headmaster of Rugby School; sought to bring religion into the daily concern of men and to invest every act of life with a Christian character. 199, 324

ARNOTT, JOHN (1940–) Born in Toronto, Canada, where he is now the Senior pastor of Toronto Airport Christian Fellowship which he founded in 1988; special emphasis on the Father heart of God; author of a number of books including *The Father's Blessing*; television broadcaster with a worldwide evangelistic and healing ministry. 75, 332

ATHANASIUS, ST (c. 296–373) Archbishop of Alexandria, who stood alone as the 'Champion of Orthodoxy', even against the Emperor; stood against

Arianism; under his influence, the Council of Nicea acknowledged the eternity of the Word of God and the Divinity of Christ – this was at a price, though, and St Athanasius spent much time in exile in the Egyptian desert. 8, 32, 55, 283

AUGUSTINE OF HIPPO, ST (354–430) Born in Algeria; trained as a lawyer but turned to philosophy and renounced his early Christian training; after a long inner conflict (see *Confessions*), Augustine was converted and baptised in 386 and ordained in 391; returned to North Africa and became Bishop of Hippo; he was known as Doctor of Grace; few, if any, Christian writers have written with equal depth on charity and on the Holy Trinity; created a theology that has remained basic to western Christianity ever since. 3, 8, 72, 100, 138, 163, 191, 197, 219, 300, 309, 337, 352

BAKKER, THE REVD JIM (1940–) Jim was born in Muskegon, Michigan; one of the founders of Christian television evangelism in the United States; author, minister and teacher; president and founder of PTL Television Network; international itinerant evangelist; founder and developer of Heritage USA, a Christian retreat centre in South Carolina; Bakker served five years of a forty-five-year prison sentence, but was subsequently found to be innocent of the charges against him. 364

BALFOUR, DOUG (1958–) Doug was born in north London, and is now General Director of Tearfund; he has been an explorational geologist, relief worker, missionary with YWAM, management consultant and stockbroker; he is married with three children and lives in West London. 266

BARTH, KARL (1886–1968) Swiss Protestant theologian and pastor; professor at Basel; stood for the primacy of the gospel against the demands of the Nazi state. Possibly the greatest theologian of the twentieth century. 30, 131, 271

BASIL, ST (330–79) Bishop of Caesarea, theologian, monastic founder and teacher; was a bishop of remarkable ability – he distributed his inheritance to the poor during a famine and organised a soup kitchen; father of Greek monasticism, with an emphasis on community life, liturgical prayer and manual work. 9

BAXTER, RICHARD (1615–91) Puritan pastor, serving first as an Anglican at Kidderminster, England, before rejecting his belief in the episcopacy; leaned towards the Presbyterian position; wrote *The Reformed Pastor* in 1656. 189

BECON, THOMAS (1512–67) Protestant divine; fellow student and friend of Hugh Latimer; wrote against corruption in the Church and campaigned for the Bible to be accessible to people; Becon's writings were banned and he spent time in the Tower of London; became chaplain to Archbishop Cranmer at Canterbury. 330

BENEDICT, ST (480–543) Born in Italy, lived as a hermit, then became abbot of a monastery and established twelve more monasteries including Monte Cassino; founder of the Benedictine discipline for monastic life – accepted throughout the West as centres of learning, agriculture, hospitality and medicine, adaptable to the needs of society. 309

BENN, THE RT REVD WALLACE (1947–) Born in Dublin, Wallace has ministered in England for twenty-eight years, including as vicar of St Peter's, Harold Wood; he is currently Bishop of Lewes; convention speaker, including at Spring Harvest; author of *The Last Word* and *Jesus our Joy*; passionate about mission and Bible teaching. 148

BERNADINE OF SIENA, ST (1380–1444) Orphan, brought up by his aunt; when he was twenty, he took charge of the local hospital during the plague; became a Franciscan Friar, and a popular preacher in Italy based in Milan; drew very large crowds for sermons that were three to four hours long, and which resulted in numerous conversions; described as a second St Paul; devoted to the Holy Name of Jesus, he used the letters IHS as Greek 'shorthand' for 'Jesus – Son of God – Saviour'; turned down three bishoprics. 85–6

BERSIER, EUGÈNE (1831–89) Minister at L'église de l'étoile, Paris; pastor and writer. 307

BEWES, THE REVD RICHARD (1934–) Richard was born in Kenya – his parents were missionaries; he entered the Anglican ministry and pastored at Harold Wood; Emmanuel, Northwood, and is currently Rector at All Souls Church, Langham Place; he is married with three grown-up children, and fits tennis and photography around his work of preaching, broadcasting and writing. 80

BONHOEFFER, DIETRICH (1906–45) German Protestant theologian, influenced by Karl Barth; opposed Nazism from 1933 and returned to Germany from the UK to train pastors for the Confessing (anti-Nazi) Church; involved in a plot to assassinate Hitler; executed in 1945; became famous for his *Letters and Papers from Prison*. 169, 233, 307

BOOK OF COMMON PRAYER Worship and liturgy book of the Anglican Church, compiled by Thomas Cranmer during the Reformation. 87, 119, 143, 155, 205, 213, 302, 310

BOOK OF CONGREGATIONAL PRAYER, 1920 Prayers and orders of worship for Congregational Churches. 31, 140, 147, 221, 258, 297, 308

BOOTH, WILLIAM (1829–1912) Converted at the age of fifteen; Methodist minister – established a mission in London's East End that was later called the Salvation Army; separated from Methodism; campaigned to alert the nation to child prostitution and child labour; established hostels and rescue houses; published *In Darkest England and the Way Out* in 1890. 143

BOWRING, CELIA (1952–) Celia was born in Tripoli, Libya; she is married to Lyndon and they have three children; Celia writes the *CARE Prayer Guide*, articles in Christian magazines and Bible notes, and is the author of *The Special Years: An Essential Guide for Parents of Under Fives*. 154, 349

BOWRING, LYNDON (1948–) Lyndon comes from Caerphilly, Wales, and was an Elim Pentecostal minister as part of the team at Kensington Temple until 1985; then he became Executive Chairman of CARE, an organisation seeking to encourage and serve the Church to engage in Christian caring, campaigning and action. 155, 230

BUCHANAN, THE REVD ALEX (1928–) Born in London, Alex has been minister or elder in several churches of various denominations: Brethren, Baptist, City Mission, FIEC, and Anglican; Leader of Intercessors for Britain and a leader of Intercessors International; author, minister at large, pastor to Spring Harvest; describes himself as 'one of God's errand boys'. 162

BUCHANAN, PEGGY (1934–) Peggy was born in Buxton, Derbyshire, is married to Alex, and is a mother and grandmother; she was formerly a schoolteacher, but became ill with MS in 1965; currently she is a Spring Harvest speaker and travels and shares with Alex in his ministry. 201

BUXTON, DAVID (1964–) Born in west London, David became the first deaf Borough councillor and the first born-deaf parliamentary candidate in the UK; he is a leader of organisations for the deaf in Britain, such as Breakthrough Deaf-Hearing Integration and Christian Deaf-Link UK; he travels, preaches and teaches the Bible in the UK and overseas. 298

CAIN, DR PAUL (1929–) Paul was born in Garland, Texas, and started preaching the gospel at the age of nine; he loves preaching the prophetic gospel – the power of God unto salvation (Rom. 1:16); he is one of the so-called Kansas City Prophets. 186

CALTHROP, THE REVD GORDON (late nineteenth century) Vicar of St. Augustine's, Highbury, and author of the devotional books called *Family Prayers* and *The Gospel Year*. 83

CALVIN, JOHN (1509–64) Brilliant teacher of Reformation theology, developing Luther's Reformation ideas; based at Geneva, Switzerland, which he decided to turn into an exemplary Christian city 'to nourish and nurture the exterior service of Christ'; his works include *The Institutes of the Christian Religion*, published in 1536. 11, 73, 174, 259, 263, 302

CAMPOLO, DR TONY (1953–) Taught sociology at university level for over thirty-five years; evangelist and leader of the mission organisation EAPE/Kingdomworks, which has developed an array of ministries in urban America and in developing countries. 93

CAREY, THE MOST REVD AND RT HON. GEORGE (1935–) Born in Bow, east London, Dr Carey has been Archbishop of Canterbury since 1991; formerly Principal of Trinity College, Bristol and Bishop of Bath and Wells. 1

CARMINA GADELICA A collection of prayers from the Highlands and islands of Scotland. 222

CASSIDY, DR MICHAEL (1936–) Michael was born in Johannesburg, South Africa; trained at Cambridge and at the Fuller Theological Seminary in California; founder and International Team Leader of African Enterprise,

which seeks to train others to evangelise the cities of Africa through word and deed in partnership with the Church; evangelist, teacher and ministry of reconciliation; his books include *Chasing the Wind* and *Bursting the Wineskins*. 331, 338, 358, 366

CATHERWOOD, SIR FRED (1925–) Sir Fred was born in Castledown, Northern Ireland, and has been involved in business and public service with the UK government; he was elected to the European Parliament, has been President of the Evangelical Alliance since 1992, and Vice-President of the International Fellowship of Evangelical Students since 1991; his books include *A Better Way – The Case for a Christian Social Order*. 356

CHALKE, THE REVD STEVE (1955–) Steve comes from Croydon, and is the founding Director of the Oasis Trust, which he set up to make Christianity relevant via social action, training and resourcing the Church; a regular broadcaster on television and radio, he is also author of many books, including *More than Meets the Eye*. 351

CHAMBERS, OSWALD (1874–1917) Preacher, teacher and writer; his many books are the result of his wife's shorthand notes of his lectures and addresses; he died while working with the YMCA among troops in Egypt. 57, 99, 134, 217, 268, 304, 321

CHARTRES, THE RT REVD RICHARD (1947–) Chaplain to Robert Runcie, Archbishop of Canterbury, 1980–84), Professor of Divinity at Gresham College, Bishop of Stepney, and then Bishop of London since 1995. 357

CLEMENT OF ALEXANDRIA (*c.* 150–*c.* 220) Born into a pagan family, but thirsted for truth; argued that the Christian truth was a superior form of philosophy while rejecting agnosticism; became head of the Catechetical school of Alexandria. 124

CLEMENT OF ROME, ST (d. *c.* 101)

Believed to be the fourth Bishop of Rome; his letter of rebuke to Christians at Corinth over immorality established some authority at Rome; possibly martyred under Domitian. 141

COLLYER, ROBERT (1823–1912) Born in Yorkshire, Robert worked in the local mill as a child and became the town blacksmith in Ilkley; he emigrated to the United States in 1850, was involved in the US Sanitary commission, and pastored churches in Chicago and New York. 223, 289, 297, 350

CONFEDERATE SOLDIER Attributed to an unnamed soldier just before the final battle of Richmond in which he died. Prayer submitted by Senator Max Cleland, Democrat of Georgia, USA. 48

COWPER, WILLIAM (1731–1800) Born at Berkhampstead, Hertfordshire; for most of his life he suffered bouts of acute suicidal depression; John Newton had Cowper (pronounced Cooper) to live and help in parish work at Olney for nineteen years; wrote poems and sixty-eight hymns which were published with those of the Newtons in the *Olney Collection* – including 'There is a fountain filled with blood' and 'God moves in a mysterious way'. 157

CRANMER, ARCHIBISHOP THOMAS (1489–1556) Favoured by Henry VIII after giving him matrimonial advice, and then promoted to Archbishop of Canterbury; introduced Reformation ideas into Anglican worship and practice; compiled the *Book of Common Prayer* in 1549; sentenced for high treason under Queen Mary and burned at the stake with Nicholas Ridley, his chaplain. 33, 123, 231, 281, 288, 311

CROSBY, FRANCES JANE 'FANNY' (1820–1915) Though blind, she taught English and history at New York Institute for the blind and wrote over 9,000 hymns, including 'Blessed Assurance' and 'To God be the Glory'; dedicated her life to serving the poorest and neediest – most of her income from writing went towards this work. 248

CYRIL OF ALEXANDRIA, ST (c. 376–444) Born in Alexandria, Egypt; considered the most outstanding theologian of Alexandria; known especially for his work on the doctrines of the Trinity and the Person of Christ; stood against the heresies of Nestorius. 269

DAWSON, GEORGE (1821–76) Pastor of small Baptist chapel at Rickmansworth before shooting to fame as minister of the Church of the Saviour, an independent church in Birmingham; internationally famous for his lectures; though not considered bound by any creed, his prayers demonstrate a devout and reverent mind. 50, 132, 165, 188, 238, 246, 287

DEARMER, JESSIE MABEL (d. 1915) First wife of the Revd Percy Dearmer; died while serving with her husband in Serbia. 82

DEARMER, THE REVD PERCY (1867–1936) Percy was born in London; he ministered at Primrose Hill up to the First World War, when he and his wife, Mabel, served with the British Red Cross in Serbia; later work included the YMCA in France, Mission of Help, India, and canon of Westminster Abbey; authority on worship and writer of hymns, including 'He who would valiant be'. 345

DEKKER, THOMAS (1570–1632) Playwright during the reign of James I; *Prayer for a Soldier* was possibly republished by him; having been written originally by someone else. 251

DIMITRI OF RASTOV, ST (1651–1709) Russian bishop; celebrated as a preacher and writer. 171

DOBSON, DR JAMES (1936–) Dr Dobson was born in Louisiana, in the United States, and is founder and president of Focus on the Family, an evangelical organisation devoted to the preservation of the home and spread of the gospel; widely recognised as a leading authority on today's family; he is also an author and television presenter; his books include *When God Doesn't Make Sense*, *Straight Talk to Men*, and *Parenting Isn't for Cowards*. 108

DRAKE, SIR FRANCIS (c. 1539–96) Born in Devon, he received an appointment 'among the seamen in the King's Navy to read prayers to them' and was ordained a deacon, taking holy orders based near Chatham; he then became a privateer, the first Englishman to circumnavigate the globe and, as Elizabeth's Vice-Admiral, he defeated the Spanish Armada. 27

DUDLEY-SMITH, THE RT REVD TIMOTHY (1926–) Born in Manchester, he has been an Anglican minister in Erith, Bermondsey and Norwich, and Bishop of Thetford; editorial secretary of the Evangelical Alliance and Editor of *Crusade Magazine*; author and hymn-writer, whose hymns include 'Tell out my soul the greatness of the Lord'. Some of the prayers listed here have been abbreviated with the author's permission. 2, 74, 208, 229, 290

DYE, THE REVD COLIN (1953–) Colin was born in Kenya and is senior minister of Kensington Temple and leader of the London City Church, one of the largest in the UK; he has a passion for reaching the lost and seeing them discipled into a strong and lasting faith. 156

EARECKSON TADA, JONI (1949–) Joni was born in Baltimore, Maryland; paralysed by a diving accident in 1967, she is now a writer, singer, and convention speaker; she is known world-wide for her work among children and adults, inspiring millions to trust in God and his sovereignty. 104

EDWARDS, THE REVD JOEL (1951–) Joel was born in Jamaica, and was appointed General Director of the Evangelical Alliance in 1997; previously he had been a probation officer

and General Secretary of the African and Caribbean Evangelical Alliance; he is an ordained minister of the New Testament Church of God, and is married with two children. 245

ELLIS, RUFUS J. (1819–85) Missionary to Bengal; wrote a manual of Christian duty called *The Light of Life*. 211

EPHREM THE SYRIAN, ST (c. 306–73) Christian poet who wrote over one thousand works involving over three million lines; defended the faith against gnosticism and Arians; died while ministering to plague victims. 196

ERASMUS, DESIDERIUS (1467–1536) Although he was Dutch, Erasmus was based in Basel, Switzerland; compiled the first edition of the New Testament in Greek with a Latin translation and notes (which were affixed to the reading desk in many parish churches by royal edict; sympathetic to the Reformation; described by Luther as 'our future and our hope'; never separated from Rome, though it was said that 'Erasmus laid the egg and Luther hatched it'. 78, 136, 159, 172, 242, 269

EVERARD, GEORGE (nineteenth century) Vicar in Dover, Southport and Wolverhampton; wrote several devotional books and compilations. 71

FÉNELON, FRANÇOIS DE SALIGNAC DE LA MOTHE (1651–1715) French bishop, respected for his learning and piety; critical of the coercion of Huguenot converts. 24

FISHER, JULIA (1952–) Born in London, Julia is a writer and broadcaster; she is currently a presenter and features editor with London's Premier Radio. 336

FORSTER, ROGER (1933–) Roger was born in London, and became the founder and leader of the Ichthus Christian Fellowship and co-founder of March for Jesus. He is also Vice-President of the Evangelical Alliance and of Tearfund; his interest in students is reflected in his one-time vice-presidency of the University and

Colleges Christian Fellowship. 200

FRANCIS OF ASSISI, ST (*c.* 1181–1226)
After a career as a soldier, he established the Franciscan order; he was committed to alleviating poverty and he initially ministered to leprosy victims; he preached a spiritual rather than a physical crusade after being disillusioned by the behaviour of the Crusaders. 107, 206

FULLER, THOMAS (1608–61) English clergyman and writer; chaplain to Charles II, best known for his *History of the Worthies of Britain*. 128

GELASIAN SACRAMENTARY (*c.* 490) Compiled by Gelasius, Bishop of Rome, who composed many prayers and revised many that were already in use. 19, 172, 187, 276, 284, 331, 353

GRAHAM, BILLY (1918–) An American Baptist preacher who had developed a worldwide ministry by the 1950s through mass crusades in various stadiums and major convention halls; books, magazines, radio and television established him as an international figure; he is also a confidant of film stars and American presidents; he is thought to have preached to more people than any other evangelist. 1

GREEK LITURGY Liturgy of the Greek Orthodox Church, originating from the third century. 76

GREGORY OF NAZIANZUS, ST (*c.* 329–*c.* 390) Theologian and Doctor of the Church; known for his work on Origen's works and also as Bishop of Constantinople; preferred an ascetic, monastic life to public life. 243

GREY, LADY JANE (1537–54) Great grand-daughter of Henry VII; Queen of England for nine days, but forced to abdicate in favour of Mary Tudor and was then imprisoned in the Tower of London; beheaded with her husband, Lord Dudley. 139

GUYON, MADAME JEANNE MARIE-DE-LA-MOTHE (1648–1717) French mystic and writer; born in Montargis, France; wanted to become a nun but was instead married unhappily at sixteen and widowed at twenty-eight; devoted her life to the poor and needy and to piety, and became the centre for the pious movement known as Quietism; imprisoned in the Bastille for her beliefs. 229

HACKING, THE REVD PHILIP (1931–) Born in Blackburn; Anglican minister in Edinburgh and Sheffield; he was Chairman of the Keswick Convention 1984–93 and is currently Chairman of Reform and Word Alive. 354

HAGGAI, JOHN EDMUND (1924–) Founder of the Haggai Institute, a unique provider of advanced leadership training to leaders in over 150 developing nations; his vision for world evangelism has taken him around the globe more than 80 times. 319

HALL, THOMAS (1610–65) Born in Worcester, he became a nonconformist pastor and writer based at King's Norton. 52, 60, 158, 239, 303

HAMMARSKJÖLD, DAG H. A. C. (1905–61) Born in Jonköping, Sweden; he served as Chairman of the Bank of Sweden, Swedish Foreign Minister and, in 1953, Secretary-General of the United Nations – a role he described as 'the curator of the secrets of eighty-two nations'; during this time he was especially involved in peace negotiations in the Middle East and the Congo. 214

HARE, MARIA (1798–1870) Wife of an Anglican clergyman at Alton and, after widowhood in 1834, based at Herstmonceux, Sussex; letter-writer and devout Christian. 270

HAVERGAL, FRANCES RIDLEY (1836–79) Born in Astley, Worcestershire, a child of the rectory; scholar, poet and hymn-writer, whose hymns include, 'Lord, speak to me that I may speak', 'Take my life and let it be …' and 'I gave my life for Thee'. 284

HENRY, MATTHEW (1662–1714) Born in Shropshire, and became a Presbyterian

pastor in nearby Chester; preacher,
writer and biblical commentator, he
is best known for his magnum opus:
Exposition of the Old and New Testament. 13, 92, 160, 209, 249, 326, 363

HENRY, DR CARL F. H. (1913–) Theologian, author, editor and lecturer;
Carl was born in New York city, and
became a newspaper reporter and editor before becoming a Christian and
turning to theology; he served at the
Eastern Baptist, Northern Baptist and
Fuller Theological Seminaries; he is
the founding editor of *Christianity
Today*, and author of more than forty
books including the six-volume work
God, Revelation and Authority. 165, 234

HENRY VI (1421–71) Born at Windsor,
son of Henry V; became king in 1422
as an infant; known as the 'Royal
Saint' due to his piety – however, his
inability to govern led to the War of
the Roses; in 1461 he was deposed and
exiled; he was restored briefly, but later
murdered in the Tower of London;
founder of Eton and King's College,
Cambridge. 132

HIGHAM, THE REVD W. VERNON (1926–)
Vernon was born in Caernarfon,
Wales, and left teaching to become a
pastor in the Presbyterian Church of
Wales; he ministered in a mining town
and in the mountains, and has been
pastor of Heath Evangelical Church,
Cardiff, since 1962; the hymns he has
written include 'There is a rock on
which I stand' and 'Great is the gospel
of our glorious God'. 212

HOW, THE RT REVD WILLIAM WALSHAM
(1823–97) Born at Shrewsbury and
entered the Anglican ministry, ministering at Kidderminster, Shrewsbury,
Whittington and London; he later
became Bishop of East London, where
he was loved for his work among the
poor, and Bishop of Wakefield; an
author and hymn-writer, his hymns
include 'For all the saints' and 'O
Word of God Incarnate'. 37

HUDSON TAYLOR, JAMES (1832–1905)
Born in Barnsley, James became a
missionary in China and founded the
China Inland Mission (CIM), later
known as the Overseas Missionary
Fellowship (OMF), the largest
Christian missionary organisation
in China and the precursor of 'faith
missions'. 276, 305

HUGHES, THE REVD SELWYN (1928–)
Born in Glamorgan, Wales; founder
and Director of Crusade for World
Revival (CWR), which is dedicated to
encouraging prayer for revival and
daily Bible reading; author for over
thirty years of the daily reading notes
Every Day with Jesus; developed
CWR's counsellor training programme
internationally. 21, 122, 176, 301

HUME, CARDINAL GEORGE BASIL
(1923–99) Born in Newcastle-upon-
Tyne; trained as an English
Benedictine monk and became abbot
of Ampleforth in 1963, then the
Roman Catholic Archbishop of
Westminster in 1976. 47, 197

HUNTER, JOHN (1849–1917) Trained at
Mansfield College, Oxford, he became
Congregational minister of the King's
Weigh House, London; preacher and
writer. 87

IBAIM, AKANU Nigerian Christian. 178

IGNATIUS OF LOYOLA, ST (1491–1556)
Spanish soldier; while wounded he
read the life of Christ, and was
inspired to an intense life of discipleship; became a religious leader, founding the Society of Jesus (Jesuits); sent
missionaries to Japan, India and Brazil;
founded schools for children; opposed
the Reformation. 49

IOANNIKOS, ST (*c.* 752–846) Greek
ascetic; following a career as a soldier,
Ioannikos became a monk at Mount
Olympus in Bythinia (Asia Minor /
Turkey); he was an opponent of the
Iconoclasts. 31

JACK, VICTOR (1937–) Victor was born in
Saxmundham, Suffolk, and has been an

evangelist with Counties' Evangelistic Work and Director of the Christian centre Sizewell Hall; in the year 2000 he became the Chairman of the Garden Tomb Association, Jerusalem, and the occasional chaplain of the tomb. 323, 344

JAMES, WALTER (1879–1908) Born in Portsmouth; a Wesleyan Methodist minister, James died after only fifteen months in the ministry; an original, vigorous and picturesque preacher, much acclaimed by all; he pastored in Lewisham, Kensington and Surrey. 38, 65, 117, 161, 265, 314, 332

JENKS, THE REVD BENJAMIN (1646–1724) Rector of Harley, Shropshire, and chaplain to Earl of Bradford; he wrote a popular family devotional book. 202, 274

JOHN, J. (1958–) J. John comes from London, is a speaker and writer, and is married to Killy; they have three sons; J. John says, 'I love Jesus and enjoy life, leisure, food and movies.' 280

JONES, THE RT REVD JAMES (1948–) James was born in Glasgow and became a teacher and co-founder of the first Volunteer Bureau in England; he jointed Scripture Union, in audio-visuals, before entering the Anglican ministry; he has served in Bristol and Croydon; he was Bishop of Hull and, since 1998, has been Bishop of Liver-pool; a writer and broadcaster, he is married to Sarah and has three teenage daughters. 262, 366

JOWETT, THE REVD. JOHN H. (1863–1923) Known in his day as 'the greatest preacher in the English-speaking world', born in Yorkshire, he entered the Congregational ministry and min-istered at Carrs Lane, Birmingham (after R. W. Dale), New York, and then at Westminster Chapel, London; his writings include *God our Contem-porary* and *The School of Calvary*. 22, 54, 216, 274

KEMPIS, THOMAS À (c. 1379–1471) Born

in Kempen, Prussia, he entered the monastery of Mount Saint Agnes where he spent most of his life copying manuscripts and giving counsel; he is author of *Imitation of Christ*, a devo-tional treatise. 20, 79, 146, 183, 255, 285, 329, 343

KEN, THOMAS (1637–1711) Born in Little Berkhampstead, Hertfordshire, he was Bishop of Bath and Wells and also a hymn-writer; his hymns include 'Awake my soul', 'Glory to Thee my God this night' and the doxology 'Praise God from whom all blessings flow'; he refused to take the oath of allegiance to William of Orange in 1688. 42, 141, 361

KENDRICK, GRAHAM (1950–) Graham comes from Northamptonshire and is a well-known worship leader and com-poser; his songs and hymns are sung around the world and include 'Shine Jesus Shine', which is currently the UK's most popular contemporary worship song. 275

KENNEDY, DR D. JAMES (1930–) Dr Kennedy was born in Augusta, Georgia, is senior minister of Coral Ridge Presbyterian Church, Fort Lauderdale, Florida, and the founding president of Evangelism Explosion International; chancellor of Knox Theological Seminary; television and radio broadcaster. 64

LACEY, GRAHAM FERGUSON (1948–) Graham comes from Solihull; he is an entrepreneur and lay preacher involved in several inspirational worldwide projects; he was the princi-pal mover behind 'The Millennium Chorus', Graham Kendrick's work for the Millennium; Graham lives with his wife, Susan, and their sons, Luke and James, in the Isle of Man. 333

LARCOMBE, JENNIFER REES (1942–) Jennifer was born in London, spent eight years in a wheelchair while her six children were still small, and received wonderful healing through prayer in 1990; she has written twenty-two books including *Beyond Healing*; she works for the organisation Beauty from Ashes, whose aim is to help those suffering from trauma and loss. 7, 89, 142, 254

LAWRENCE, BROTHER (seventeenth century) Born in France, he was converted at the age of eighteen and later became a monk with the order of the 'Discalced Carmelites'; he is best known as the author of *The Practice of the Presence of God* in which he sets out his spiritual principles: an over-whelming delight in God and the practice of deep submission to God. His real name is Nicolas Herman. 68, 213

LITURGY OF GENEVA (first printed *c.* 1542) Originally adapted from Martin Bucer's German by Calvin. 135, 318, 330

LITURGY OF ST MARK Used at Alexandria and named after St Mark; now generally assigned to the fourth century or later. 84

LITURGY OF SYRIAN JACOBITES (third century) Liturgy of the Syrian Jacobite Church; all Syrian Jacobite liturgies are thought to be derived from St James; 'James' being 'Jacob' in Greek. 166

LLOYD-JONES, DR D. MARTYN (1899–1981) A Welshman with a brilliant medical career ahead of him, he answered God's call to the ministry in 1923 as pastor in the Welsh Calvinistic Methodist Church; characterised by a remarkable openness to the Holy Spirit, he has been described as the greatest theologian-preacher since the Puritan John Owen; he served as a minister at Westminster Chapel between 1939 and 1968, initially as Campbell Morgan's associate, and rapidly became the natural choice as minister to students; his expository sermons – for example, *The Sermon on the Mount*, *Romans* and *Ephesians* – are still being published. 61, 175, 355, 360

LONGFELLOW, HENRY WADSWORTH (1807–82) Born in Portland, Maine, in the United States; Professor of Modern Languages and Literature at Harvard; best known today for his poems 'The Wreck of the Hesperus', 'The Village Blacksmith', 'Evangeline', and 'The Tale of Hiawatha'. 56

LUNN, THE REVD SIR HENRY S. (1859–1939) Born into an old Lincolnshire Methodist family; entered the Wesleyan Methodist ministry in 1882 and spent a year in India before his time there was curtailed by ill-health; the controversies he raised regarding missionary policies in India led to his resignation from the ministry; organised ecumenical conferences in Switzerland which led to the foundation of the Lunn travel company; joined the Anglican Church in 1910; wrote *The Love of Jesus*, a manual of prayer, meditation and preparation for Holy Communion, in 1911. 98, 134

LUTHER, MARTIN (1483–1546) German reformer; as Professor of Biblical Exegesis at Wittenberg, he opposed corrupt practices of the Church and preached the doctrine of salvation by faith alone – nailing his ninety-five theses to the Wittenberg church door, he started the fire of the Reformation; 'He possessed the power of kindling other souls with the fire of his own convictions.' 125, 224

LUTHERAN SERVICE BOOK Prayers and orders of worship for Lutheran Churches. 210

MARSHALL, PETER (1902–49) Born in Coatbridge, Scotland, Peter served in the British Navy but sensed a call to the ministry; he graduated from Columbia Theological Seminary, Georgia, was pastor of New York Avenue Presbyterian Church, Washington, DC and, in 1948, became chaplain to the American Senate; he wrote *Mr Jones* and *Meet the Master*, and was the subject of the book and film *A Man Called Peter*. 10, 128

MARTIN, SAMUEL (1817–78) Born and raised in Woolwich, south London, Martin became the first minister of Westminster Chapel at the age of twenty-five; he was widely respected for his preaching but he also had a great concern for both the young and the poor of the Westminster slums, and inspired his congregation to be involved in caring for the poor; friend of Lord Shaftesbury. 103, 228, 310

MATHESON, THE REVD GEORGE (1842–1906) Church of Scotland minister in Edinburgh; almost totally blind, but was an academically gifted church historian and theologian; able to memorise sermons and entire sections of the Bible – listeners were often unaware that he was blind; wrote hymns, including 'O love that wilt not let me go' and 'Make me a captive, Lord'. 101, 181

MCNEE, SIR DAVID (1925–) David was born in Glasgow into a Christian home, and has always had involvement in the Scottish evangelistic movements, including Tell Scotland; and served as chairman during Billy Graham's mission in 1991; joined the police force in Glasgow in 1946 after war-time service in the Royal Navy, becoming Chief Constable of Glasgow and then Strathclyde, and finally Commissioner of Police of the Metropolis (London). 315

MELANCTHON, PHILIP (SCHWARZERD) (1497–1560) German Protestant reformer, associate and fellow worker with Luther; composed the Augsburg Confession (1530); led the Reformation movement after Luther's death; wrote *Loci Communes* in 1521 – the first great Protestant work on dogmatic theology. 25, 110, 177

METHODIST BOOK OF OFFICES, 1936 Orders of service for the Methodist Church, which draws on Christian

devotion through the ages. 69

MORGAN, DR G. CAMPBELL (1863–1945) Campbell was born in the afterglow of the 1859 Revival, and by his early twenties had an international preaching ministry; in the United States he was seen as D. L. Moody's successor; in London, where he was minister of Westminster Chapel (1904–17 and 1935–43), he was spoken of as successor to Spurgeon; his books are still popular, especially in the United States. 325

MOTYER, THE REVD ALEC (1924–) Born in Dublin, Alec first sensed a call to the ministry at the age of six, though he was not converted until he was fifteen; has ministered in Wolverhampton, Bristol, London and Bournemouth, before teaching Hebrew and Old Testament at Clifton, Tyndale Hall and Trinity Colleges in Bristol; he is a writer, convention speaker and specialist on Isaiah. 263, 291

MOZARABIC LITURGY The ancient liturgy of Spain until the eleventh century. 60, 220

MURRAY, ANDREW (1828–1917) South African religious leader and writer; ordained into the Dutch Reformed Church, he became an itinerant evangelistic preacher after revival broke out in his parish; he placed an emphasis on prayer and personal holiness, and wrote *With Christ in the School of Prayer* in 1885; also concerned for the welfare of Africans, he opposed Afrikaner nationalism and British colonialism. 149

NESTORIAN LITURGY Named after Nestorius (d. 451), a zealous ascetic; Nestorians are concentrated in Kurdistan, Iraq and (a few) in India. 62

NEWMAN, JOHN HENRY (1801–90) Born in London, he became a preacher and founder of the Tractarian movement; became a Roman Catholic priest in 1845 and established the Birmingham Oratory; appointed cardinal; wrote the hymn 'Lead Kindly Light' and 'Dream of Gerontius' – the latter was set to music by Elgar. 4, 91, 170, 244, 296, 334, 347

ORIGEN (c. 185–253) Born in Alexandria and became head of the Catechetical school there at the age of eighteen; a preacher and teacher, he opened a school at Caesarea, but suffered during persecution under Decius; the first systematic theologian, Origen sought to establish a reliable text of the Old Testament, and is known especially for his *On First Principles*. 43, 153

THE ORTHODOX WAY CHRISTMAS DAY VESPERS A book about the Greek Orthodox Church, its doctrines, discipline and devotional life; written by Bishop Kallistes Ware. 226, 359

OULD, THE REVD FIELDING (d. 1864) The vicar of Christ Church, Hunter Street, Liverpool, he is especially known for Trinitarian teaching. 67

PALAU, LUIS (1934–) Luis was born in Buenos Aires, Argentina; he committed his life to Christ at the age of twelve, started preaching at eighteen, and had a tent and radio ministry by his twenties; the Luis Palau Evangelistic Team has an international preaching ministry – 13 million in sixty-eight nations to date, and even wider radio and television work; he is also a prolific writer, whose books include *Where is God When Bad Things Happen?* 267

PARSONS, DIANNE (1949–) Born in Cardiff, Wales, and married to Rob, Dianne works with Care for the Family and is the presenter of 'The Issues Women Face' seminar series. 335

PARSONS, ROB (1948–) Rob was born in Cardiff, Wales, and is Executive Director of Care for the Family; he is the author of a number of books including *The Sixty Minute Father*, *The Sixty Minute Marriage* and *The Sixty Minute Mother*. 340

PASCAL, BLAISE (1623–62) Born in Clermont-Ferrand, France; French mathematician, physicist, theologian and philosopher; his experiments with mercury led to the invention of the barometer, hydraulic press and syringe; he patented a calculating machine and his studies led to the invention of the integral calculus; his *Pensées* [*Thoughts*] show profound thought on Christian truth. 96

PATRICK, ST (c. 385–c. 461) Born in Scotland of Roman Catholic parents, but kidnapped and sold into slavery in Ireland; his experiences led to spiritual discovery and he became a missionary; appointed Bishop to Ireland, he preached to thousands, mainly in the spiritually barren areas in the north and west, establishing communes; he wrote *Epistola* in which he contemplated the ill-treatment of Irish Christians by the British. 77

PATRICK, BISHOP SYMON (1626–1707) Bishop of Ely. 149

PERRY, RT. REVD JOHN (1935–) John was born in Mill Hill, London, and has been vicar at St Andrew's, Chorleywood, warden of Lee Abbey, Bishop of Southampton and, since 1996, Bishop of Chelmsford; he is author of *Effective Christian Leadership* and has a wide involvement in the Christian healing ministry. 194

PHILARAT, METROPOLITAN THEODORE (1553–1633) Metropolitan Bishop of Moscow. 18

POLYCARP (c. 70– c. 155) Possibly a disciple of St John; Bishop of Smyrna (modern Izmir); especially known for his martyrdom – when invited to recant, he replied, 'Eighty-six years I have served Him and He has done me no wrong; how then can I blaspheme my King who saved me?' 195

PRAYERS FOR SOCIAL AND FAMILY WORSHIP Prayers prepared by the Church of Scotland in 1862. 106, 127, 203, 241, 318

PRIME, THE REVD DEREK (1931–) Derek was born in London, and has served as pastor in Lansdowne Evangelical Free Church, London, and in Charlotte Chapel, Edinburgh; since 1987 he has devoted his time to writing and an itinerant ministry. 63, 120, 167, 312, 341

PROCTER, ADELAIDE ANN (1825–64) (Pseudonym – Mary Berwick) English poet, born in London; contributed to Dickens's *Household Words*; her poems include 'The Lost Chord', set to music by Sir Arthur Sullivan. 204

PUSEY, EDWARD BOUVERIE (1800–82) English theologian and leader of the Oxford Movement; born in Pusey, Berkshire; Religious Professor of Hebrew at Oxford; translated Augustine's *Confessions* and the works of Tertullian; built churches in east London and Leeds. 5, 59, 113, 166, 227, 261, 317

RAUSCHENBUSCH, WALTER (1861–1918) Born in Rochester, New York; an American clergyman; Professor at Rochester Theological Seminary; leader of the Social Gospel Movement, stressing social issues as being one of the purposes of Christianity. 179

REDPATH, ALAN (1907–89) Left a successful career in business at God's call to be an evangelist and Bible teacher with National Young Life Campaign; became pastor of Duke St Baptist Church, Moody Memorial Church, Chicago, and Charlotte Baptist Chapel, Edinburgh; was widely known as a conference speaker and writer. 194

REES, TOM (1911–1970) International Bible teacher and evangelist, writer and broadcaster; conducted United Church campaigns and organised camps for boys from the slums; emphasis on reaching university students; filled Royal Albert Hall over fifty times; committed most of the Bible to memory. 225

REYNOLDS, BISHOP EDWARD (1599–1676) Bishop of Norwich,

remembered for moderate treatment of dissenters; involved in Savoy Conference, 1661; Wesley included some of Reynold's sermons in his Christian library for his preachers. 28

RICHARD DE WYCHE OF CHICHESTER (c. 1197–1253) Born in Droitwich, son of a yeoman farmer; Chancellor of Oxford and Chancellor to the Archbishop of Canterbury; regarded as a model diocesan bishop – charitable and accessible, generous to the poor during times of famine. 34

RIDLEY, NICHOLAS (c. 1500–55) Born near Haltwhistle, Northumberland; his various posts included chaplain to Thomas Cranmer and Henry VIII, Bishop of Rochester and Bishop of London; he helped Cranmer prepare the Thirty-nine Articles of the Church of England; on the death of Edward VI he denounced Mary I and Elizabeth I as illegitimate, and espoused the cause of Lady Jane Grey, but was executed when Mary became Queen. 100

ROMAN BREVIARY The book of prayer for the Roman Catholic Church, compiled over many centuries; in its full form it runs to several volumes, and was originally published in Latin. 206

ROSSETTI, CHRISTINA (1830–94) English poet; born in London, the sister of Dante G. Rossetti; her hymns include 'Love came down at Christmas' and 'In the bleak mid-winter'. 27, 44, 50, 94, 105, 115, 171

ROWLANDSON, MAURICE (1925–) Born in London, Maurice was called to 'full-time' Christian work at Keswick; he trained in Minnesota when Billy Graham was president of his college and has worked with him since; secretary of the Keswick Convention, magistrate, lieutenant commander in the Royal Navy Reserve; author; founder and president of the Venturers' Norfolk Broads Cruise for Youngsters. 137, 286

RUSSELL, GEORGE (1935–) George comes from Edinburgh and is in business in the private and public sectors; he is actively engaged in Christian interests such as CARE, Mission Scotland and Allander Evangelical Church, Milngavie; he lives in Glasgow with his wife Moira – they have three children and two grandchildren. 173, 295

SANGSTER, THE REVD DR WILLIAM EDWIN (1900–60) Methodist minister renowned as an evangelist, preacher and writer; he ministered at Scarborough, Leeds and Westminster Central Hall where he served Londoners through the Blitz by visiting the shelters; twice he was president of the Methodist Conference; known nationally for a sermon he gave in 1952, entitled 'A Sermon to Britain', about the moral condition of the land; he was convinced of the need for revival. 243

SCRIPTURE UNION PRAYERS FOR SCHOOLS, YOUTH GROUPS, CHURCH SERVICES AND PERSONAL USE A collection of prayers compiled by Godfrey Robinson and Stephen Winward, and published in 1967. 22, 35, 40, 192, 242, 272, 320

SERAPION (d. c. 350) Bishop of Thmuis (or Thumis) in the Egyptian delta; a contemporary of St Athanasius and St Anthony. 58, 157

SHAFTESBURY, LORD (1801–85) Seventh Earl of Shaftesbury, also known as Lord Ashley; English reformer and philanthropist, involved in factory, housing, army schools and mines reform. 26

SLATER, RICHARD (1854–1939) Father of Salvation Army music, a 'pioneering giant' of the Salvation Army; also a prolific song-writer, writing the lyrics and/or music of a total of 851 songs – 587 of them published during his lifetime; served at Regent Hall, Hoxton, Tottenham, New Barnet and Wood Green. 55

SPURGEON, CHARLES H. (1834–92) English Baptist preacher; born in Kelvedon, Essex; pastored at the Metropolitan Tabernacle, seating 6,000; emphasis on the evangelical nature of the Baptist Union, which led to his separation from it in 1887; prolific writer; he established a training college for young preachers and an orphanage. 16, 90, 130, 168, 207, 232, 273, 279, 322, 365

STEVENSON, ROBERT LOUIS (1850–94) Scottish writer born in Edinburgh; afflicted by constant illnesses, including tuberculosis; famous for his books: *Treasure Island*, *Kidnapped*, *Catriona* and *The Strange Case of Dr Jekyll and Mr Hyde*; also wrote a book of prayers while travelling in Samoa. 119, 182, 327, 343

STOBART, THE REVD HENRY (c. 1820–90) Graduating from Oxford in 1847, Henry served in the Church of England from 1849 to the 1880s and was Rector of Warkton near Kettering 1865–81; author of *Daily Services for Christian Households*. 345

STOTT, DR JOHN (1921–) John was born in London; was Rector of All Souls Church, Langham Place, London from 1950 to 1975, and is now Rector Emeritus there; he has written a number of books, including *Basic Christianity*; he was appointed honorary chaplain to the Queen in 1959. 12, 54, 272

STOWE, HARRIET (ELIZABETH) BEECHER (1811–96) American novelist, born in Litchfield, Connecticut; raised in a puritanical family and married a theologian; famous for *Uncle Tom's Cabin*, published in 1852. 17

SURSUM CORDA Latin for 'Lift up your hands'. Four-line exhortation as part of the liturgy at the start of prayer. From the Anaphora of St Mark, a primitive liturgy from the second century. 294, 328

SYMEON, ST (949–1022) Known as the

New Theologian; Byzantine monk and mystic; prayer was very important in St Symeon's life; he was abbot of St Mamas monastery, but the monks rebelled against his austere regime; he put emphasis on individual experience, and believed that all Christians are capable of knowing God directly through prayer. 70, 152

SYNESIUS OF CYRENE (b. *c.* 375) Pagan intellectual who became a Christian in order to serve the Christian society of his day; strenuous defender of his flock. 102

TAYLOR, JEREMY (1613–67) English theologian, born in Cambridge; chaplain to Archbishop Laud; imprisoned during the Civil War; became Vice Chancellor of Dublin University and a member of the Irish Privy Council; his writings are considered to be among the most eloquent sacred writings in the English language. 29, 133, 240, 292

TEN BOOM, CORRIE (1892–1983) Dutch evangelist and author; helped 700 Jews escape during the Second World War, which led to her imprisonment in 1944; following her unexpected release from Ravensbrück, she established a rehabilitation home for concentration camp victims in Holland and a home for refugees in Germany; her books include *The Hiding Place* and *Tramp for the Lord*. 23, 62, 66, 102, 183, 195, 214, 241, 248, 273, 286, 342

TERESA OF CALCUTTA, MOTHER (1910–97) Born in Yugoslavia of Albanian parents; she became principal of a convent school in India, but left the convent to work in the slums of Calcutta; she opened a Home for the Dying in 1952 and founded the Order of Missionaries of Charity, which is now at work in 200 houses in several countries. 352

TERESA OF AVILA, ST (1515–82) Born in Avila and sent to a convent at sixteen, she became ill and partially paralysed for several years, but saw visions of Christ which strengthened her spiritual life; she founded thirty communities for women and also ones for men. 25

TERSTEEGEN, GERHARD (1697–1769) Born at Mews, Prussia; German preacher; pastor and prolific hymn-writer; experienced revival in his church at Mülheim in 1751; his hymns include 'Lo, God is here!', 'Let us adore' and 'God reveals His Presence'. 293, 353

THORNHILL, THE REVD ALAN F. (1908–) Chaplain of Hertford College, Oxford. 260

THORNTON, HENRY (1760–1815) Member of Parliament, philanthropist and economist; influential member of Clapham Sect alongside Wilberforce; supported anti-slavery campaign, and was also involved in the Church Missionary Society, and the British and Foreign Bible Society; gave away over 80 per cent of his income; he has several publications to his name, including a book of family prayers. 121, 150, 220

TILESTON, MARY (d. 1895) Compiled devotional books. 53, 76

TOPLADY, AUGUSTUS MONTAGUE (1740–78) English Calvinist clergyman and hymn-writer; born in Farnham, Surrey; vicar of Broadhembury in Devon, and preacher in the Orange Street Calvinistic Methodist chapel near Leicester Fields, London; his hymns include 'A Debtor to Mercy Alone' and 'Rock of Ages'. 44, 95, 185, 299, 308

TORRANCE, PROFESSOR THOMAS F. (1913–) Born in China of missionary parents, Professor Torrance lectured in Church History and Christian Dogmatics at Edinburgh University; especially concerned to root students in Reformed dogmatics and to introduce interest in the Greek Orthodox Church; moderator of the General Assembly of the Church of Scotland; awarded the Templeton prize. 25, 66, 240, 291, 346

TUTU, DESMOND MPILO (1931–)
Desmond was born in Klerksdorp in North-West Province, ordained an Anglican priest in 1960, and has been Dean of Johannesburg, Bishop of Lesotho, and the first black General Secretary of the South African Council of Churches; awarded the Nobel Peace Prize in recognition of 'the courage and heroism shown by black South Africans in their use of peaceful methods in the struggle against apartheid'. 6, 8, 118, 236

WASHINGTON, GEORGE (1732–99) Born in Virginia, in the United States and the richest man in the land; rose through the ranks of the British army in the Colonies and defeated the British forces with the aid of France in 1781; he retired from the army to form a government; he drew up the American Constitution and became first President of the United States. 53

WEATHERHEAD, DR LESLIE (1893–1976) Methodist minister at Manchester, Leeds and London (City Temple); popular Christian writer and academic, with a special interest in psychology and the healing power of prayer and faith; Weatherhead spoke to men and women in their difficulties, and understood suffering having served in the army during the First World War; his books include *A Private House of Prayer*. 36, 40, 68, 111, 288, 313

WESLEY, JOHN (1703–91) Born in Epworth, Lincolnshire, son of a rector; at Oxford he headed a pious group nicknamed 'The Holy Club' or 'Oxford Methodists'; he discovered the failings of piety as a missionary to Georgia and experienced the assurance of salvation by faith in a Moravian meeting in 1738; he travelled 250,000 miles on horseback, preaching 40,000 sermons; though he sought to be loyal to the Church of England, Wesley was forced to break and form his own societies that later became known as the Methodist Church. 51, 198, 244

WESTON, THE REVD CANON KEITH (1926–) Keith was born in Croydon, Surrey, and ministered in St Ebbe's Church, Oxford and as Honorary Canon of Christ Church Cathedral, Oxford; has also been an international speaker and Chairman of the Keswick Convention; he is married to Margaret, and has four children and seven grandchildren; though retired, Keith is still busy preaching. 276, 306, 348

WILLIAMS, ROWLAND (1817–70) Tutor at King's College, Cambridge, and Professor of Hebrew at St David's Theological College, Lampeter; known in his day for his studies on Christianity and Hinduism; contributor to the controversial *Essays and Reviews*; recognised for his integrity and search for the truth. 81, 256, 278, 316

WIMBER, JOHN (1934–97) John came from Peoria, Illinois, and was a professional jazz and pop musician; he received Christ in 1963 and became an evangelist and Bible teacher, placing an emphasis on evangelism and healing called 'Power Evangelism'; he was the founding director of church growth at the Fuller Institute of Evangelism, became leader of the Vineyard Christian Fellowship, and established an international ministry through writing and conferences. 10, 32

YONGGI CHO, DR DAVID (1936–) David was born in Kyungnam, Korea, and has become pastor of the world's largest church, Yoido Full Gospel Church, Seoul, which has more than 770,000 members; he is especially known for his teaching on the power of positive faith, prayer, principles of church growth and home cell groups. 218

Index